also by sarah arvio

*Sono: Cantos*

*Visits from the Seventh*

night thoughts

# night thoughts

70 dream poems & notes from an analysis

## sarah arvio

Alfred A. Knopf  New York  2014

Grateful acknowledgment is made to Random House, Inc., and Curtis Brown, Ltd.,
for permission to reprint an excerpt from "Lullaby (1937)" from *Collected Poems of
W. H. Auden* by W. H. Auden, copyright © 1940 and renewed 1968 by W. H. Auden.
Used by permission of Random House, Inc., on behalf of North American print rights
and Curtis Brown, Ltd., on behalf of UK print and world electronic rights.

Special thanks to Victoria G. Pearson

Library of Congress Cataloging-in-Publication Data
Arvio, Sarah, 1954–
Night thoughts : 70 dream poems & notes from an analysis / by Sarah Arvio.—1st ed.
p. cm.
"This Is a Borzoi book."
Includes index.
ISBN 978-0-375-71222-7
1. Dreams—Poetry. 2. Women Poets, American—20th century—Biography.
3. Dream interpretation. 4. Psychoanalysis. 5. Memory. 6. Women's dreams.
7. Language and languages in dreams. 8. Psychic trauma in adolescence. 9. Young
women—Sexual behavior. I. Title.
PS3601.R78S66 2006
811'.6—dc23    2012020095

Jacket image by Malin Gabriella Nordin
Jacket design by Elena Giavaldi

Manufactured in the United States of America
Published January 9, 2013
First Paperback Edition, August 6, 2014

*for Rigel*

Nights of insult let you pass
Watched by every human love.

—W. H. Auden

# contents

## notes

### figures  86

# a word to the reader

*night thoughts* is an exploration of the dreaming mind. It is also an intimate memoir, describing the evolution of a psychoanalysis and the events that gave rise to that treatment. It gives the reader a set of dream poems, then notes and an index of images.

Although the dream poems are best read sequentially, they may also be read by dipping in and out. The notes, however, should be read as a narrative, from start to finish.

The index offers a way to relocate or cross-reference some of the images, colors and other dream-related thoughts that occur and recur in the poems and notes.

S.A.

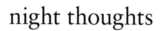

night thoughts

poems

# oh hell

there are still the bad dreams I have to say
a dram in the thought of a bad bad night
a bad potion potent with impotence
& pain that dream in which you say I
am ruined with you I am no more &
the taxi leaves me standing in the street
& the streetlamp goes out there is this sort
of dream that leaves me without a heart or
more like with a hole in my selfheart
heartself that hellhole of a dream
oh hole oh hell the inside of my mind
damning me with bad portents & potions
you said to come I came & you killed me
this kind of killing that kills me again

# snakeplant

I have a snakeplant spiking from my skull
with a slim yellow stripe on every spike
I have dirt falling through my yellow hair
& jade rings on my toes on all my toes
in all the shades of jade of snaky jade
that smack as I walk on the wooden floor
I am self-repulsed & reptilian
jaded shady I am not me I am
a jade I say a spike a spiky jade
I am yellow but not curious all fear
all sallow callow damp in wet green jade
I don't think I like myself this smacks
of snake this smacks of musty mossy damp
oh say I say this smacks of me of me

# altar

there's an altar on the altiplano
all white stone under an altering sky
& pink water is running down through a sink
this is the white sink of the sacrifice
bloodwater the water is mixed with blood
& I'm washing water down the sink
there's a finger left from the sacrifice
one baby finger lying on the stone
it isn't my finger it is someone's
whose name is young beautiful or else young war
& she doesn't have a hand or a head
or a body she's nothing anymore
alone on the stone alone on the stone
she's lying altered on the altarstone

# snakes

I stand at the mirror  at the mirror
I'm standing staring at myself not
my self but my slight slim girlbody
standing at an angle & here I am
with the old brownpaper wall behind me
when the snakes begin to swarm in the brown
roses behind me then push out lifting
their heads & snaking out & then I turn
& run with my hair flowing behind me
up the pair of stairs & down the long hall
down the long front stairs & over the porch
along the brick walk & across the lawn
as they snake behind snaking as snakes do
but flying also brown like brownpaper—

8

# white hat

I'm out walking in a white shirt white skirt
white hat under some trees   when I come out
into the sun & away from the trees
all my white clothes are splashed with blood
I feel no sense of drama or surprise
no shock there is only this thought my white
clothes are splashed with brightpink blood as though
splashed with the shadows of the trees I don't
say pink in the dream I don't say shadow
or white hat   only later thinking back
I notice that the blood is prettypink
gaudy & there is noplace it comes from
it is mine or not mine but from noplace
I know of  out walking in a white hat

# airplane

& now an airplane lands in the field
& incinerates I use this strange word
when I tell the dream   not flames or burns
there was a rusty barrel out in back
we called the incinerator strange word
for an old barrel where we burned the trash
I took my diaries out there in back
in the brightdamp where a spatter of rain
fell in the ashes & striking matches
lit the edges & watched as the pages
curled charred & would not burn I said my life
burn up my life & for one lifetime
I thought I can stop now & take them back
but no they were burning so I let them burn

# spoons

& now I will marry & I open
the silverdrawer but the silver spoons
are snapped at the neck they lie there snapped
in the bed of the drawer like the silver
heirloom rings our grandmother gave us
made of her old spoons inscribed with the names
of old aunts & I wonder what happened
to the bowls of the spoons maybe they spooned
together like lovers do lying in drawers
but without their hafts or they rolled over
in sleep spoonfeeding love maybe they were
spoonfed all the love a lovespooner needs
& the looming of my nevermarriage
her silver hair my yellow hair our hearts

# forsythia

here's a dream about my mother there are
three black smokestacks in a black night sky
belching black smoke & yellow sparks &
as the sparks land beyond the black river
they are yellow forsythia blossoms
cynthia was my mother so ha ha
we said for cynthia for cynthia
to the great bush of flaming yellow sparks
only now years later I say for sin
then incinerator for the barrel
where I burned up my sins I had tried to
insinuate myself into her thoughts
but no luck they were elsewhere but why three
black smokestacks & why the black river

# robin's egg

I want to make love with you on the porch
the shady porch with windows all around
& the maple trees all leafy all around
everyone is coming onto the porch
they won't let us have our love embrace
there's a girl named robin carrying an egg
a toy egg called a robin's egg & she
smiles demurely as she gives me the egg
it's skyblue as sky as spotted as a
robin's egg & just as breakable as
I knew   I had seen a tiny half egg cracked
with a tiny creature coiled up inside
it had fallen from the maple tree & cracked
& the realbaby robin chick had died

# red buick

there's an old red buick on a mountain
& a red phone   in life the redphone was
in the hall & the realgirl robin phoned
& said we heard you did something that
begins with F & ends with U–C–K
& it's not FIRETRUCK I spelled it out
& thought is that what I did or did not
or else maybe almost FIRETRUCK UCKFUCK
& I heard her laugh & another girl
laughed years later I saw her & she said
we were all doin' it you were too young
my softsillyself taking the redphone
hearing the firetruck & burning red
alone redface on the mountain alone

# sugar

in this dream a red truck an old red truck
with some bold gold letters across the side
SUGAR TRANS____ATION COMPANY is it
transubstantiation or translation
but no the missing word is only port
I think there's no importance to this dream
I think what matters is what it's porting
or will it translate me to somewhere else
maybe it's the place of all the sugar
& who it ports it to is only me
who needs more sugar than she knows she needs
sugar if only someone would say it
in the ports of my ears sugar sugar
this would be the sugar of the red truck

# three fish

the mother of the boy I will marry
she takes the knife & she turns it over
on the cutting board beside the white fish
laying potato peels over the fish
each white fish is striped with one red stripe
the red stripe marring its delicate flesh
my white dress is spattered with brightpink blood
all the white lace is spattered with my blood
she hides the three fish from the wedding guests
covering them up with potato peels
she's hiding the fish from their fish shame
she doesn't hide me I can't hide myself
she hides the three fish so no one can see
covering them up with potato peels

# squirrel

then I remember that I once cut off
the tail of a squirrel I hauled from the woods
thinking of something that was kittensoft
I laid it on my mother's cutting board
it was big dank dead & fur gray stiff
why did she let me cut the tail on her
cutting board I didn't like it it was
hard inside & the fur was rough I had
to bear down & grind I didn't like it
but had begun & so went on   I saw
the fur teacup in the glass case   when I
sipped I gagged this was not surrealism
it was super real it made me hot & bored
squirrelism it made me squirrel inside

# cats

in the next dream there are four cats or three
& now the three cats lap milk from a dish
while the fourth cat swells large & on his nose
spots pop out he's a wildcat he steps through
a window onto a roof & the sash
drops on the mount of his tail & lops it
I say that's my mom she's leaving us she
wants to be a man she's a manxman but
a long time later I know it's him he
was my catpal among the catpals &
then he catapulted me into wild
catland where the spots were in my eyes
oh catpot of milk I was kittened in
& my mom was sashaying somewhere else

18

# watermelon

in the brightwhite kitchen a tiny pink
watermelon lies on the pink counter
or white it may be white but the fruit
is pure pink flesh I take a bite of it
then I recall a photograph of me
standing & biting the watermelon
in the newspaper that was black & white
though I know my shirt was white & pink
at the fair on something hill (named for
a fruit) where my father bought me a book
that was called something hill something that meant
flesh & then I knew it was fanny hill
the place was strawberry hill & little
me as francesca seduced by a book

# pink pistachios

I'm lying naked on a field of ice
no not naked I'm in a black teddy
with redpink flowers while the sun sets
smearing its penetrating pink & red
on my limbs & ass & on the ice
& tom a boy stands gazing there's a bush
with bare branches & pink pistachios
all over it big & pink & open
I say piss & mustache that's my dad
the nuts are a man's sex but we know this
& nuts are nuts we all know what this means
& bare & pink this would be my wish
& ice is my ass & ice is my soul
& a tom is a boy but we know this

# catwalk

in this dream there's a secret walkway
hung high around the room all the way up
near the ceiling we climb there in secret
I call it a catwalk a place where cats
go stealthily there are some folks below
laughing & clapping who don't know we're up
here above as though we were in heaven
to you I say we're secret lovers now
& then forever after this is true
I love but only in secret or not
at all & mostly not at all   now I
remember that in the room where we played
there were ladders horizontal high up
I walked with the cats & that was how

## suitcases

I can't find any mention of this dream
in my notes but I know I had it
I am climbing in the roman ruins
on a sloping hill & I carry
two suitcases or maybe three but no
I couldn't manage three they are leather
& ladylike & delicate one pink
& one white the sun is burning goldhot
on the sloping hill goldhot on the stones
it strikes me that my diaries were pink
& white there were two or three fauxleather
with small gold keys & gold trim & gold lines
on the page where I scribbled my young words
those were the diaries I later burned

# escalator

too many dreams in this one I'm riding
up an escalator & I step off
onto a gold carpet near some gold drapes
I wonder why the gold why all that gold
& years later after many long thoughts
I know that in the room where we lay down
there was a goldcolored modernist couch
& some nubby gold curtains & a streak
of light shone through them our skin was whitepale
golden the skin of children touched by sun
this is the way of the dreams here I am
riding up up up a lifetime later
& I step off & nothing happens
just a cheesy giltgold department store

# pale blue sheets

the señora is turning back the sheets
& showing me the spots of freshred blood
near the pillow on the pale blue sheets
as blue as sky I write this in my notes
but out the window the sky is white
what language do you speak she says   I don't
I say—which seems to mean I really do—
& later I remember the toy egg
nesting in the hand of the girl robin
who hands it to me with her girly smirk
pale blue & spotted like the pale blue sheets
& pale blue like sky or not like sky
& now I have no language I can speak
the señora is turning back the sheets

# letter

there was no dream about the letter
my father sent or my father didn't send
the letter that may have said it happened
no one told me what the it of it was
all I knew was they were reading the letter
wherever people were the letter was
being read & then being read again
& there was the red shame of being read
as in the joke black & white & red
which was the blushing zebra of my shame
or the newspaper splashed all over
or else the bleeding nun or the red ink
bleeding into black ink on the old manual
where all letters written were also red

# black chairs

I sit in a row of black foldout chairs
on a checkered floor big black & white checks
I have a big white bandage on my hand
my right hand the thumb & first & middle
are wrapped in white gauze now my hand falls off
no not my hand only the bandaged part
it rolls there crooked on the checkered floor
now someone laughs now all the others laugh—
I cut my finger I had a black & white
checkerprint dress I knew I would be cut
I watched my finger fold before my eyes
my life fold in fold out before my eyes
they fixed me up with black thread white gauze
& not a laugh no not a laugh at all

# black slip

I borrow a slip from another girl
a black slip with a lace décolletage
& she accuses me of stealing it
no I say I didn't steal the slip I
borrowed it but no one believes me here
the magistrates are standing near the wall
& they sentence me to a razor death
my executioner has jetblack hair
long & skanky & it swings as he steps
toward me with the razor in his teeth
I'm sporting the black slip in which I'll die
the black slip with the lace décolletage
but then I seize the shining instrument
& zig it through the air & slash his eye

# shiny foil

a man on the ship has molested me
I say so I say he molested me
& now with the sun gleaming beyond us
& the cold sea rising & rollicking
& the ship deck heaving beneath our feet
they sentence him to sudden death at sea
& even now I see the razor blade
shimmering like a slip of shiny foil
& giving us back all the shining sea
it scrapes across his throat & so he dies
his head lurches back & his soul leaps out
No I say he only molested me
with all the love that I was longing for
but it is far too late to mollify

# quarrel

here's my squirrel that's now become a rat
or become two rats or there may be more
in a glass cupboard turning round & round
in a quarrel a quarrel of squirrels
showing their teeth I feel queasy & sick
the rat with the head of a squirrel or
the tail of a squirrel I don't know which
did I mention that they're all white pure white
the cupboard lying flat and the white cups
falling off the cuphooks as they scramble
I'm afraid that if I open the glass door
they will enter me & become me or
isn't it true that they already are
I made them in my dream with all their teeth

# glass case

in a wooden shop spare & quakerish
I'm standing near the glass pastry case
& inside the case there are stacks of shit
laid in a row on some small white plates
I've got to shit & put it in the case
but I don't know how to get a plate or
how to put the plate in the pastry case
my skirt hoisted in front of the glass case
I try squatting but no way to do it
while thinking about cakes & confections
joseph beuys comes to mind his sausages
lying old & crinkled in a glass case
& the glass incubator inside of which
the long confection of my life began

# cary grant

my mother has been chopping people up
in my dream & hanging them from poles
cary grant hangs from a shower pole
without his thumbs & toes he doesn't care
but that's because he's dead but I do care
the shower curtain is yellow dingy
& the light too bright glaring on me
dear mother is it thumbs up or toes down
I'll sit down on the edge of the bathtub
& cry I'll sit & see if I can cry
do you care will you grant me a wish
will you grant me one of your kisses
caring or not caring these are the poles
will you shower me please with affection

# snake vacuum

in the hallway the super has a snake
vacuumcleaner meaning she holds the snake
by the tail & it sucks up dirt & dust
through its mouth while slipping across the floor
a black snake very long & big around
now it climbs up inside my legging up
one leg & down the other cleaning me
but I don't feel clean I feel filthy
with the thick black creature under my pants
moving slowly & using its sharp tongue
to tickle me there are the garbage cans
& the mailboxes I don't think I love
my life or any life or life at all
here filthy in the hallway of the dream

# big empty bed

a big empty bed with a canopy
over it & some white sheets & in them
under the top sheet I find his penis
not much like a penis it isn't smooth
but here it is lying all alone &
I wonder where he is & why he has
left it here to be found by me & why
I have found it here alone without him
& how he feels without it in his pants
I stick it in my pocket what else can I do
& feel it there all ropy & estranged
& grieve for our estrangement & his loss
& for my finding what is still our loss
& for the empty sheets where I find it

# lips

another night I find lips on my chest
they're near the middle on the left-hand side
wings I think & then I see they're fleshy
not mouthlips these are the lips of the sex
I see that my sex is right there on my chest
like wings but fleshy & with an open place
I think that would mean leading to the heart
then I think yes that's where the lips should be
the problem is that when I wear a blouse
they make a lumpy place over my breast
& I can't keep people from noticing
you can wear your heart on your sleeve but not
your sex on your heart & next time I look
they're flitting around like a butterfly

# button

I find a navy button on ninth street
& third avenue lying on the street
& it belongs to a navyblue suit
threepiece pinstripe & with a navy shirt
I once wore to the beach over blue jeans
some sailors on the beach accosted me
highwind blueclouds highwhitewaves highbluesky
all highwhiteblue & me filled with blue fear
of the sailors walking along the beach
the sailors in their white hats on the beach
my hair blew whitegold in the blue air
I felt goldwhite fear when they looked at me
there was nowhere to hide in the blue sky
& the white gulls were diving & rising

# poker

banners are hanging from the picket sticks
bearing royal heads from a pack of cards
down the dusty path under the trees
there once was a poker game with the king
the only hands that touched the cards were his
one was the queen card I was the queen
then he left the room with a poker face
he left me with jack meaning with nothing
the jack who jacked me up against the wall
& who poked me & played me & poked me
& here they are the royal brothers' heads
riding on their banners through my dream
on the dusty picket under the trees
& all I wanted was the royal kiss

# snakes

they rubbed my back with something like snakes
& those were their own snakes rubbing me
snakes that I could never have seen
they rubbed me with something like fingers
but couldn't exactly have been fingers
as I wept & leaned against the furnace
standing & weeping as they rubbed me
rubbing the points of their snakes into me
so that they entered the inner realm of me
revolting me as though they had been snakes
& in fact they were snakes rubbing me
snakes of the aggressive thanatos
not even of the temptation or garden
undulant as a dream but they were not

# pain

there was no pain in the dreams there was no
pain in the night dreams but in the day dreams
there was no dreaming there was only pain
there was no pain meaning the dreams didn't hurt
it was the waking that hurt with dreams in it
it hurt from the dreams that didn't feel pain
but the dreamer felt pain on waking up
the parts of bodies on the bathroom floor
the sudsy filthy water on the floor
ask if you clean your body with the dirt
& yes you clean your body with the dirt
you wash the parts of your one soulbody
with the dirty dirt of your memories
then leave them lying on the bathroom floor

# master bed

in the master bed of my childhood house
I am lying in crumbs dirt & debris
& I roll over toward my analyst
who's getting in the bed just now with me
into the vile bed where I lie with me
into the big bed where my parents lay
getting into the bed with me but why
I say why are you getting in with me
who am so dirty sick & vile who am
so sick in mind & dirty in body
how can you love me if I am so vile
but why he says why are you vile & yes
I say why am I vile & all the while
I am brushing the dirt from my body

# rock

you can sleep on a rock my mother says
standing beside a flatfaced rock is that
the rock I can sleep on is that the rock
she's tall & flatfaced standing by the rock
with some light passing around her body
& marking the trees in the winter woods
I know I feel stricken & desperate
though there are no feelings inside the dream
I know because I would feel this in life
if she told me I could sleep on a rock
a hard place to sleep a rock it could hurt
it could hurt for days & maybe for years
lying on that rock & bruising myself
for I slept on the rock & I was hurt

# war

high over the hudson in an L-shaped
room there are plateglass windows all around
& a war  in the war a blond woman
whips a razor through the air   no that's not
it   I'm the blond woman & I'm the one
that whips it I slash her lean tan face I
don't ask why a razor there have been too
many & I don't ask why a blond I
am a blond I don't say why a war I
know there's a war instead I say what
is the L the L is love & the war
is being fought in the L of love high
over the river where love laps & flows
& high in the air where love laps & flows

# razor

she wakes in the night to a razor cut
guillotine or scissor or knife or sword
cutting fingerneckthighbreast lipofsex
as freud said was it the fear or the wish
& who is the cutter & who is cut
the cutting words prefiguring the act
in the wordmind where the thoughts are made
little wordrealm where the word is the sword
her mind that will always be somewhere else
her mind that will never be anything else
despite the blandishments of all of life
& all life embellishments cut away
by a secret cutter with a secret act
& nothing but a dream to figure it

# stone well

& now I recall the first badblood thought
that was not a dream but could have been
there was a well at the back of our house
near the stone wall & salvia & sedum
a deep old well with a stone over it
a flat stone that was too heavy to lift
when I saw the razors begin to wing
in a swarm of blades that were flatdark wings
in a swarmstorm in a deepred cloud
through the stiffsharp air so close to the house
I got the stone from the back of my mind
& rounded up the razors with the stone
steered them to the well & trapped them there
laid the stone on them & tried to forget

# cord

here I trip on the cord of the iron
as I skip across his mother's kitchen—
what did I burn?—it was the pale blue shell
a gift when I turned twelve I wore it once
burned it with the iron & tossed it out
on a day with no irony or sky
but now I know the secret of the shell
some words from the dream of the toy egg
come to me as though the sky opened up
pale blue shell that was the robin's egg
the egg & the shirt have the same name
a pale blue shell that lost its baby bird
& iron is the burning irony
& the cord is the cord of the mother

# V

she burned her shirt in the shape of a V
& what was the V not victory
& not vagina   that was too easy
but the triangle appears in the night
on tiny pillboxes & escutcheons
as insignia on blue dishes & jewels
the triangle of the mons veneris
to the mind of a tiny girl no the girl
was not tiny but her knowledge was
& now these triangles that appear
in jeweled form inhabit her nights
with their ancient symbology the girl
could not know but she knows the shape
of her new mound the one venus cares for

# sphinx

the darkhaired girl is a beautiful sphinx
egyptian sphinx crouching in the desert
with her darkblack cleopatra eyes
her bigcat ribcage is flayed to the ribs
& between the ribs she's flayed away too
the desert wind blows on her flayed ribs
the pain of the flaying blows through her ribs
it whistles this flaying pain it almost sings
with the sandsharp sting of the desert sand
crib of her crouching & secret knowing
in the sand sphinxdom of her suffering
patria of her desert suffering
she turns her bigcat eyes to me & speaks
she speaks to me I don't know what she says

# leopard

the leopard girl lands & she takes a turn
in the leafy woods she leaps & she lands
she is a leaper as I also am
look at her redbreasts as she takes the turn
those are my breasts I say to my mother
or as though to my mother who is dead
shiny red satin she wears on her breasts
under the spotted cape that flings out wide
who is the redhaired redbreasted leaper
all burning up in her greengirl joy
a leaper of a girl that's what she is
coy bravura the joy of her breasts
look how she glitters in her coyjoy
how brave she is in her red satin breasts

# red satin

I'm in a red satin dress with red lace
there are two men   I don't know which is mine
the penis of one man sticks straight up
through the flaps of his hangingout shirt
I don't know which man is the other man
there's a black rotary phone & a wad
of black opium I buy a dollar's worth
the poppyblack looks nice with red satin
I smoke & smoke in my red satin
It's a red dress I sat in as I smoked
the other man I don't know what he does
I keep the black wad resting on my lap
the opium on my red satin lap
like the poppy with its opiate heart

# corner

I meet my love it's not night & not day
at a table not indoors or outdoors
the sky is a ceiling or the ceiling sky
all in purple silver there is no wind
he says he bought a house on the corner
for us for our life bought us a house
I look & look there is no corner
the houses are a seamless silver row
purple & silver & deepforest green
it opens & shuts like a paper fan
as for me I haven't got a corner
he's leaving me now to sleep on a slope
his corner is on a slippery slope
all around there are forests & forests

# three chinese jars

my door is ajar & so I go in
man in the apartment how did you get in
easy he says there are keys in the jars
in all three chinese white porcelain jars
no point saying that the jars are inside
& that the lock on the door is outside
jarring to find you here I think I say
a damn chinese puzzle I think I say
I found my door ajar that's how I'm in
he found a dream door that's how he got in
I thought you said you found keys in the jars
keys in the chinese blue porcelain jars
I found the keys in the jars of your heart
everyone knows a key goes in a lock

# green snake

enter apartment with a box of snakes
& the phone rings   put the box down
a green snake crawls out with a big belly
sticking up boxy green with red markings
the snake is pregnant I say in the dream
a lot like the hat of the little prince
that was pregnant with the elephant
pick up the phone  another snake crawls out
man on the phone   a man I never met
I say come over & help me with the snakes
& then I'm waiting but he never comes
green red pregnant it could be anything
a week ago the snakes were long & black
& slithered on the refrigerator

# three vases

the three glass vases standing in the hall
in a last ray of summer evening light
each of the vases holding three roses
drowning underwater the three roses
yellowrose pinkrose & also bluerose
down in the water their fullpetal heads
that flow a little like little girls' hair
in the dark hall in a last ray of light
we were three little girls is that the three
I was born third on the third of a month
on the wallpaper were three old roses
over & over the same old roses
the dreamdrowning flowinghair roses
& in the dream a ray of evening light

# fruit bowls

fruit bowls in the middle of a table
have yellow & red & blue fruit in them
I remove three large pieces of excrement
from my body & wrap them up like fruit
in tissue paper  I remove the pieces
in an abstract way & without disgust
as though they were fruit & then I
wrap them like fruit   remembering the dream
I feel a real & non-abstract disgust
at me for dreaming of my excrement
although in the dream it is delicate
& almost sweet as though it were the fruit
& yet I know the meaning isn't sweet
or yellow red or blue or beautiful

# tulips

I apply for a competitive job
in the first cut I receive three flowers
three paper cutouts of flame-red flowers
flame-red flame-red flame-red & all cut out
they are tulips or else parrot tulips
I have two lips this is what I know but
here in the dream I have the three tulips
my two lips speak & when they speak they flame
& when they flame they are parroting me
they may be me speaking back to myself
a bright green parrot speaking with my lips
they could be saying I know you're cut out
for the flame-red parrot tulip job or
could be saying I know that you were cut

# sheer

there's a girl wearing a see-through blouse
the man says you're wearing a she-through blouse
& she says I didn't know it was sheer
the next time she looks her breasts are sheared off
this is sheer agony that's all it is
the big shears lying in the back of her self
& here she is she-through showing herself
all through & through he sees her & she sees
herself cutting herself sheer to the nub
the blouse is sharing something that she has
a beautiful soft offering she has
& here is the nub of the truth of it
why would she shear off the beauty she has
who can never see herself through & through

# shoaling

& then another dream at crystal lake
in the shallows where I've been wading
late in the day under a strange dusk light
a blur of small white fishes ripples by
& now I see the tiny drowned babies
lying on their sides & streaming by me
sheathed in tiny scrolls of toilet paper
that flutter behind them as they swim
but I still know nothing I don't know why
the babies would be drowned or why they wear
toilet paper around them as they swim
shoaling & hurrying like sperm or why
the strange low light or why they are shoaling
in the lit shallows of my rushing mind

# causeway

on one side a lake with smooth water
on the other a sea of rough water
falling off deep from the side of the road
& the yellow rays of the evening sun
in the dark deep I'm rocking underwater
I don't know why I've chosen the rough deep
down in the deep I watch a yellow ray
strike a young blond woman deeper under
she reaches for me through the rocking waves
& for her baby sinking down under
& here is the cause & here is the way
that I will save myself for she am I
reaching to me as she rocks in the waves
one side smooth water the other side rough

# olivia de havilland

I tell olivia I would rather die
than let them throw my suitcase overboard
while the boat rocks & the spray splashes up
everyone's suitcase must go overboard
but my case is more dire more desperate
because I have nothing left in the world
only my suitcase & the drenching deck
she says she will help me I weep & wail
if I lose my suitcase I'll go overboard
her last name is havilland which means
have a land meaning will you have some land
& land is what I need to do & have
I'm far out to sea on the lurching deck
I need a remedy to suit the case

# culotte

I'm wearing an olivegreen culotte dress
this is all that happens I wear a dress
later I call it the mondegreen dream
which may mean green world or else green mound
these are the mundane facts of the thought
my silver ring dropping down through a pond
dropping down through a stripe of yellow light
down & disappearing underwater
down through the cool dark olive green water
for cul is an ass & otte is a little
& sometimes a little can mean a lot
an olive may mean I'll live I will live
& a culotte is also underwear
& here is the underworld of the thought

## cactus

in another dream a weird green cactus
in the shape of a crabbed hand or the winged
victory of samothrace I sketch it
& there she is the wind the scalloped wings
the shoulderstub I had just seen her she
was on my mind they had found her right hand
but not all the fingers the thumb & ring
& were showing them off in a glass case
the ringfinger had lost & found its tip
& now my finger aches where it was cut
it almost lost its tip & then was stitched
she doesn't need her fingers anyway
she has the cactus of her great green wings
flying up behind her in victory

# bell

at the sound of the bell a big bully
with a ticker & a pulley & a chain
& a hammer & a bar & a bang
smashes the head inside the headshaped frame
time in the ticker continues to tick
the head in the frame is my own head
pale side of head like the carlo carrà
with a black background like a nightblue sky
this is the dreadful lyrical huzzah
a pale head on black turning to the side
all the bellthoughts lyrethoughts all the beauty thoughts
smashed by the bully in the big machine
I'm the head or else I'm the smasher
maybe I'm the head & the smasher both

# ropeladder

on the ropeladder hanging from the roof
hearing andrás schiff play the variations
I hang here swaying in my white chiffon
my hands above me & my hips forth
I'm hanging here & I've spread my legs
& out flies a splat a red splat of birth
that flops & slides on the toilet floor
far down below where my mother stands
throwing a shadow on the toilet floor
it looks like a red hand or red starfish
the five fingers of my shame splatted out
lurid & sumptuous in my white chiffon
I'm sloughing something but what I don't know
out of the sea dream out of the deep self

# knife

my mother comes at me waving a knife
there's a long mirror on the closet door
I'm looking in the terror mirror &
I'm thinking her knife is a rhyme for life
but this is a murderous reflection
nowhere to hide from my life or hers
nowhere to hide but in the long mirror
in the mirror where nothing is hidden
except all that is lying behind us
I don't see us I see where we once were
with our long love mirrored & closeted
& now here she is waving the lifeknife
as close as I can come to disclosure
she isn't dead there is no closing yet

## snow

I'm lying in a drift on the white road
white dark roadside in the snowingwhite snow
wearing a light slip or my nakedness
& the snowdrifts are drifting against me
in the blurring snow the whirr of some wheels
& a pair of snowslow lights are turning
I must roll over roll away & hide
my hips won't roll as I will them to roll
if they see me for sure they will hurt me
white snowslurred lights sweepstrafe my nakedness
hurt me or leave me naked in the cold
strafe my heels hips shoulders straggled hair
I'd rather be hurt than left in the cold
lovely I am turning in the snowcold

# crying

I love girls crying on station platforms
this is not a dream this is the truth
they are crying over their broken thoughts
crying over the night thoughts & the day thoughts
those are the ones they are crying over
I cry too seeing them cry & seeing
me in my life standing on the platform
crying out my eyes & down my young face
my youngold crybaby face crying out
without a sound on the station platform
or maybe with a caughtup breath & no more
though my chest goes updown as I cry in
crying over & over on platforms
wherever I am in the crying world

# mustang

a flock of giant birds all red & blue
gallop at me  three naked feathered men
mustang! comes the cry & three of them
gallop at me  three naked feathered men
lifting their legs & dancing as they come
with red & blue feathers waving behind
& all the rest of them is nakedness
& one has got a lock a giant lock
he's going to lock the sky he's got a lock
as they gallop at me crying mustang!
must hang you must hang you must hang you must
& the sky behind the lock is perfect blue
& all the red blue feathers on the ground
the lock is silver & the sky is blue

# three boys

I forgot the three boys for many years
who took me into the woods with them
or I went along with them wanting them
& they barely touched me in my terror
playing at touching as though it were done
& nothing was touched & nothing done
but I did not know that nothing was done
& I did not know for most of my life
even that I went to the woods with them
or that they had done nothing to me
& when I remembered I saw the leaves
that were brown & knew it wasn't spring
& saw the light that was not spring light
& my jacket that was dirtied by leaves

# rusty

the man in the bed his name is rusty
the last name sabon I know his brother
he lies on the bed showing his stiff cock
last week I hiked up sabino canyon
& saw some cardinals as red as blood
redder than blood if that can ever be
& it comes to me that my first monthblood
was the color of rust instead of blood
instead of the redfeathered cardinals
& this is a cardinal point for me
how my young blood could have the look of rust
& even the scent & tang of rust
from the dream of the man last name sabon
like the sabine women who once were raped

# hanger

an old hanger pierced my skinny body
& laid its rust in my pretty womb
& I lay loosely on the bathroom mat
my tummy valley lying smooth & flat
near the neat hill of my naked venus
& my lanky legs & my newborn breasts
& the rust lay there in my new body
the rust spread through my ancient soul
& dying turned me purplish pink & blue
& as I died I thought of me & us
& this was the rusting of my blood
in the belly of the mind of my soul
& now I have the rusted thoughts & dreams
& now I have aborted the lost tool

# south

in my dream notes there was a missing word
that belonged to a place called valley road
I wrote every thought that came to my mind
behind the lost word fell the missing clue
on south valley road was the stonewell house
& the clue to the terrible bloodthought
the thought that had been cutting up my life
& stone was what I used to hide the thought
& well was the place where it was hidden
sometime after the stabbing happened
we had often gone down the valley road
& the thought was I was the sarah slashed
& valley was the place my life would go
& going down was also going south

# eyelet

sometimes I'm wearing a white eyelet dress
that was my mother's quaker wedding dress
the eye of the cotton I have always thought
it is always bearing a splotch of blood
at least once I'm in the swingset swinging
in a chiffon dress & there is no blood
once I met the other sarah swinging
one day when I was swinging & swinging
she showed me the slash scar in her belly
it swung through me as though it were my own
this was the blood of my eye that was let
that saw the bloodletting behind the day
this wasn't something I could cotton to
though it cottoned onto me & stayed

# stone + well

& so then all at once it came to me
alan stonewell was the boy who cut her
stone + well was the bloodrazor swarmthought
& the stone was what covered up the well
& the stone was what I used to steer the swarm
the redbloodcloud & hide it in the well
stone breaks scissors & paper covers stone
in the bright moment of the revealed thought
the mindbond is broken but not the mind
the bondage to the element of thought
in the skincut & lifecut & soulcut
he cut her & it should have been me
the darkmind bloodthought shocking my mind
almost all my bloodlife & all of me

# cave

there's bright fire shooting up from my hands
along the ridge near the cave passage
near the mudred bloodred terror caveplace
the sculptural curving okeeffesque place
where in terror I know I must enter
I stand staring at what I must enter
with the bright fire shooting out of my hands
at the place that is narrower than me
opening in the mudred bloodred place
& then I sense a shift in the caveplace
& I pass through my own narrow passage
which may be a birth passage of my *me*
the birth canal was narrower than me
& yet I entered it & I went through

# end

there isn't an end this is what I know
there is no end & no bottom to it
this makes me think of the bottom of me
that is bottomlessly infinite in me
in my moods that go swinging through myself
selfmood mindself always overwhelmed
by what happened or else didn't happen
what didn't happen was that I was loved
I was bottomless in my falling down
through the bottomlessness of the unloved
the end of life I think is to be loved
or to love someone else who must be loved
that is bottomland to the bottomlife
a place to lie down & a place to kiss

notes

Many poems behave like dreams, chasing associative patterns through the mind, using riffs and non sequiturs. They draw on the unconscious mind in their development of thought patterns. A poem can be like a dream, dancing around an idea and avoiding it.

These poems, however, directly describe dreams I had long ago during a psychoanalysis and the associative thoughts that followed—as I free-associated from the dreams in my analyst's office or wrote out my dream thoughts. The dreams are inextricably linked in my mind with those thoughts.

Several years into the analysis, I began to travel often for work, and I started the practice of writing out my dream associations in longhand immediately after writing down the dreams. At first I wrote half a page, later I often wrote six pages, or seven. It usually took six pages to write out every thought and to come to something that seemed to be the dream's meaning or message. This was often a sequence of connected memories, and often alluded to the same set of traumatic events that occurred when I was eleven or twelve years old. I got in the habit of writing out my dream notes every day, even while not traveling. The order and timing of the events was a matter of intense importance—since I felt that if I knew when the events happened and in what order, I could understand how they had happened. Again and again I described the clothes I was wearing, the season, the weather, the room, the car, in an effort to establish a timeline. Sometimes I thought I had it figured out, and then the memories simply slipped.

The early dreams were utterly baffling and it was not until long afterward that their meanings began to come to me. This is true, in particular, of the dreams of blood, razors and excrement, which frightened me profoundly and seemed to have no meaning.

When I say 'the early dreams,' I mean those that came to me early in the analysis.

I had gone into therapy and later into analysis after a semi-psychotic experience—in which I imagined, while riding the subway, that my hand had fallen off at the wrist and was rolling away. Later I came to see this fantasy as a wake-up call—if I don't get help soon, I won't even be able to reach for it. I also had had, and began to have again, fantasies of being cut by razors, knives, swords—anything with a cutting edge—scissors, even pins. Most often, they struck me in my sex—and I writhed in bed, trying to bear the anguish. But they also cut my legs and hands, especially my fingers. I woke to find a guillotine or an egg slicer slicing my fingers.

The fantasies were worst when I was in a state of rest, either reading or attempting to sleep. I had to stop reading when the crowding into my mind of terrible thoughts became intolerable. I also sometimes stopped sleeping for weeks, or slept only a few hours drugged by wine, or woke clutching myself or clenching my fingers. The fantasies could also strike suddenly anywhere, in my own kitchen, in a train or a theater, or while I was walking alone on a city street.

I did not know why I was having those terrifying thoughts, and I could not control or diminish them. They might, I speculated, have something to do with my mother's unkindness, since I often viewed her comments to me as *cutting.* And yet, I saw my mother as a good mother, and myself as a failure for no reason I could identify. Quite a long time passed before I had the dream in which she instructs me to sleep on a rock, a turning point in my understanding of my life.

I even speculated that the cut attacks—my name for these mental events—resulted from my father's violent rages, which he often had while wielding a household tool: a saw, a carving knife.

Over the years I had scattered nightmares; after I began the analysis the dreams came frequently, often in linked spates or sequences, sometimes close together and sometimes months apart.

Free-associating from a dream, I worked on all the remembered parts—and sometimes, as I worked, I remembered more of the dream. Gradually, the shadows or snips of memories became fuller, more precise and more detailed. And yet, after dreaming, thinking, searching, longing, I still could not, for a very long time and then sometimes only momentarily, put the events in order or make one explain or cause the other. I did preserve a memory of the date—April 16—that I lay down with the cat—the boy I'm calling 'the cat.' I don't know how I remembered the date, except that I must have reread my diaries over and over before I burned them.

The dreams rarely referred to my present life: they drew me into the long past.

The dreams told in these poems are parts of dreams—for me the memorable and iconic parts. And then too, there is no such thing as a discrete, separate dream. Dreaming is an endless stream. I don't know where my dream begins: I dip in somewhere. I know where it ended: with my waking up. A remembered dream can be a single image, or a long complicated story.

I had many, many more dreams with similar imagery; the poems describe the dreams that seemed to matter most.

When I give the name of a dream here in quotes, I'm referring to the dream and the poem interchangeably.

All the dreams told in the poems except for "snakes" (1)

and a part of "snakeplant" came to me during the years of the analysis.

I have slightly changed words and names in some of the figures to disguise them. It's important to bear in mind that a word or name in a dream is not necessarily that word or name: it may be a clue to something else. Sometimes the person named has played a role in the creation of the troubled thoughts, sometimes the name alone (as meaningful wordplay) has importance without real reference to a person.

It intrigues me that the discoveries from the dreams occur through strings of linked thoughts. Many of these strings follow colors. Some revelations come through homonym words or phrases whose meanings are linked in the dream thoughts (like *sheer* suggesting *shears*). Some come from a name that suggests an image (*Rusty* becoming *rust*), or a name that suggests words (*Havilland* becoming *have a land*). Some from an image that suggests a name (*forsythia* calling up *Cynthia*). Or an image in the same pattern as another (a checkered floor becoming a check dress or a cactus suggesting the shape of a Nike).

By 'dream thoughts,' I mean all the thoughts that occur in the dream or arise from it.

What I'm calling a 'figure' is a striking single image, or an image that repeats itself, calling attention to its importance.

When I use the word 'memory'—or invoke the idea of memory—I'm remembering real events and also imagined real events. By this, I mean events that occur in the mind as thoughts.

I'm also remembering other thoughts, and dreams, which are also thoughts.

Memory preserves what happened in life and also what happened in the life of the mind.

Several poems are not dreams: "letter," "snakes" (2), "razor," "crying," "three boys" and "end." "squirrel" describes the memories that arose from the figure of the cutting board in the dream "three fish." "stone well," "south" and "stone + well" describe the working out of a fantasy; "hanger" another related one. "V" and "eyelet" pan several dreams. "snakeplant" combines two dreams, one long before the other; "oh hell" and "pain" talk about pain and dreaming and then turn to a dream. Many of the poems that describe dreams also tell something about the stories that lie behind them.

I often, throughout the analysis, felt that I understood certain figures and images only to have their meanings disappear again. Over and over I said to my analyst: What did that mean? What did we say that meant? I had spoken of the image, time after time, but now my mind was blank: I had lost the sense of it again.

I came to understand that the mind seeks to disguise and conceal what is too painful or shaming to endure—

and at the same time offers up clues to the secret. The clues appear in troubling dreams or disrupt the sane mind with their terrors.

## events

There were three events that tangled together to create the experience of trauma. I reconstructed them piecemeal, fragment by fragment, over a long period of searching.

ONE: An older boy, my near neighbor—whom I adored and idolized—cajoled me into playing 'strip poker' in his basement, where we sometimes played. In the poems, he is the cat; in life, he had the nickname 'the king.' The other players were my school girlfriend, who left midgame when it was time for her mother to pick her up, and the cat's younger brother and the brother's friend. After I had relinquished all my clothes, the cat disappeared upstairs, leaving me alone with the two other boys. They hid my clothing, taunted me, and rubbed my slim young back with their penises while I wept, whimpered and begged them to stop. I have no memory of having seen their penises, I recall only the sensation of snakelike objects pushing against me: dry, hot and rubbery. I was saved by the sound of a car entering the driveway. I don't know why I didn't scream—maybe because I felt that I had brought it on myself by agreeing to play the game. I didn't run because I was naked and couldn't get away without betraying myself.

TWO: Sometime around this time, I lay down with the cat on his living room couch and *almost* had sex—I might have had it, had his mother not pulled into the driveway at the moment that he was pushing the head of his penis into me. He pushed into me about a quarter of an inch, or maybe a half. . . . I don't think I knew what the sensation was, or I knew and did not know at the same time. It was ravishing, all-enveloping, soul-sweeping. It was tender, trembling and wild. And then suddenly I was crossing the driveway and hurrying home across the lawn. The result was what my analyst called 'disorganizing'—it disorganized my psyche. I had the sensation of pulsing or pounding inside me and also all around me, a kind of drumbeat taking over the world. I don't know how many hours or days this lasted.

I'm also sure I didn't go to the cat meaning to have sex: I wouldn't have been able to say what that was. I simply crept after him and embraced him. Or we rollicked around each other as children do and got caught in an embrace. I speculate that I may have wanted to reassert my love and allegiance in the wake of his brother's awful act.

THREE: Sometime also around this time, I was in the playroom of the cat's house, where lots of boys and girls were tumbling and playing. Several boys were punching me softly, pummeling me, and I entered into a dizzy eroticized state. Then I walked with them—three of them—down the hill and into the woods where I lay on the leaf-strewn ground while they playraped me—played out a gang rape. They did not even touch me, taking their little penises out of their pants and bending over me. I let them do this to me.

I believe this event came after the other two events—and was the result and expansion of my precocious, frightening and almost hallucinatory arousal.

♣

As I write this—now, years later—I say to myself, so there were *three* events, and twice *three* boys—as though it were a new discovery. But it is a new discovery, since I've never set it out before in these terms.

This is all—or almost all. A few days or maybe weeks, some trespass, some touching. And yet, powerfully distorting my young life.

I now know that it took me a year to forget—for around a year I continued to feel heart-churning anguish about these incomprehensible happenings, telling myself again and again that I had spoiled my life. And then I forgot.

I sensed that something had happened to make me wary and distant, and I experienced myself as having lost all erotic sensation. I separated from my gales of giggles, my romping and frolicking, and began a life of evasion, thrill-seeking and cynicism. I was attractive to the boys, with my bright waist-length blond hair, my pale skin and aura of cool—and I roughly rebuffed any attempts at closeness, much less love.

And later, older, I began to be sick. Sick at heart, sick to my stomach, addicted to wine and cigarettes, hopeless, and then semi-psychotic. By this word, I mean that although I knew what was real and what was not, I could not protect myself from the obsessive and terrifying fantasies.

# figures

## BLOOD, BLOOD ON WHITE CLOTHES

"altar" filled me with a cold, alienated terror, and I had no idea why on earth I would be given such a dream. I woke from it with the sense or taste of blood all around me and in me, and a kind of awe at the immense moving sky.

What have I sacrificed to the gods? Everything but a baby finger.

I must have thought of myself, at the time of the dream,

as making a kind of sacrifice to the gods: here, have all of me, but give me my life. I wonder if a person can be resurrected from a baby finger—surely the most useless part of the body.

It's clear there's not much left of the person.

At the time of the dream, I had not yet learned to free-associate· letting the mind tumble from thought to thought, word to word, image to image. Hard to learn, frightening—you don't know where you will tumble.

I have never associated the dream with my own cut finger, although there is undeniably that. The clue of the dream, which I found while writing the poem, may be in the play of *altar* and *alter*.

What I call the 'altiplano' is an immense mesa, with sides dropping steeply to a plain below.

I notice that I've described the blood on my clothes in "white hat" and in "three fish" as bright pink; in "altar" the 'bloodwater' is also pink. I have no explanation, except to refer to the pinkness riff that runs through "watermelon" and "pink pistachios."

In another dream near in time to "white hat," a large round bloodspot appears on a man's bright white shirt. He bends sideways and falls to the ground.

In another, also near in time, men stand around me, poised for attack. They haven't attacked me, but there is blood on my white clothes. Again I'm wearing all white.

In "three fish," the dress is a blue lace cocktail dress I had recently bought—transformed into a white dress. It reminded me of my mother's wedding dress, which was not lace but white cotton eyelet. She had wanted something suitably simple for her Quaker wedding.

I began to see that the blood was often or almost always on white clothes.

But there were other instances of red on white. In "three fish," there was a red stripe on the flesh of each of the three white fish.

In another dream, there were three neat stripes of blood on a toilet seat. I saw this pattern, but couldn't decipher it.

It was a long time before I considered the preponderance of threes.

'Eyelet' was also an important figure in my dreaming mind.

INCINERATOR, FORSYTHIA, IN SIN

My first real breakthrough was the dream called "airplane." Describing the explosion of the plane, I used the word *incinerate*. And then I remembered burning the diaries. When I say 'remembered,' I don't mean I recalled something I had thought of now and then over the years. I mean that the memory broke open, shocking me, and I saw that it—the event—had happened, that I had known of it long before, and then forgotten.

The sudden viewing of a lost traumatic memory happened only a few times during the analysis. 'Sudden' means shocking—the return of a powerful memory.

Other memories came more slowly.

I understood later that a traumatic memory lost and then found releases other memories.

By 'breakthrough,' I mean this was the first time I had the sense that there was more to know about my suffering and that I might be able to find it.

♥

Growing up, we lived among woods and orchards north of New York City, not far from the Hudson River.

The barrel where I burned my diaries was in our backyard, near the woods. In the dream, the airplane bursts into flame on the edge of a field near some woods.

In "forsythia," the sparks shoot from black smokestacks. These are also, in a sense, incinerators.

There was a forsythia bush in the side yard, under the pine tree—flamboyantly announcing the arrival of spring and always blooming on my April birthday. And yet, how impossible not to see that it belonged to my mother, since her name was Cynthia.

I often climbed to the top of the pine tree, so I could sway in the wind and view our yard and woods from the highest point.

The word *sin* came as a surprise, and I remembered that my mother's mother called her Cinny. The words *Cynthia* and *incinerator* combined to produce the idea of sin and living in sin—with its reference to sex.

And burning up my diaries in the incinerator: burning my sin.

In Quakerism, there is no problem called 'sin.' The notion of sin came to me from stories and novels.

The belching of the smokestacks and the blackness of the smoke also suggest pollution—. It was a black, black night, lit by shooting sparks that are blossoms. The black river is our river, the Hudson, and the sparks fall across it, from west to east, becoming forsythia blossoms on the other shore.

SQUIRRELS & RAT SQUIRRELS

Free-associating from the cutting board and kitchen knife in "three fish" brought me quickly to the memory of the large, dead (but still slightly warm) squirrel whose tail I cut off. I had carried it in my arms up from the woods and brought it through the side door into the kitchen.

My grandmother sometimes took us all, fixed up in pretty dresses, to tour the old Museum of Modern Art, where the fur teacup[Ψ] sat in a glass case in a room full of other surrealist works.[Ψ] I don't know what sort of fur it is—I haven't seen the cup for many years—but I imagine squirrel fur, gray and coarse.[Ψ] I still wonder whether my queasiness, almost nausea, on seeing it—I averted my eyes as we passed the glass display case—came before or after cutting off the squirrel's tail. *Surreal* means 'above real' or 'more than real,' and when I say *super real* I mean, by contrast, 'much too real.' I find it curious that Merriam-Webster gives *surreal* as 'marked by the intense irrational reality of a dream.'

"quarrel" spun from the squirrel memory: combining the sound of the word *squirrel* with my sense of terror

---

[Ψ] Méret Oppenheim, *Le Déjeuner en fourrure* (Fur Breakfast).

[Ψ] In the same glass case, Marcel Duchamp's *La Mariée mise à nue par ses célibataires, même* (The Bride Stripped Bare by Her Bachelors, Even), and on a plinth nearby, Man Ray's eye on a metronome (*Indestructible Object* or *Object to Be Destroyed*). These art objects are uncannily pertinent, especially if I reveal that my father, the first *man* of my life, was named *Ray*.

[Ψ] The fur turns out to be gazelle.

and chaos. The fallen teacups, I now notice, revisit the problem of the fur teacup.

The red Buick was a big convertible with its top down, dangerously perched on a mountaintop. We had a red rotary phone hanging on the kitchen wall with a red cord so long that you could get pretty far down the hall, or around the corner into the coat closet to talk on it.

The phone I answered when Robin called was a black phone in the upstairs hall. But the red phone helps to give away the dream's secret: the word *firetruck*, the taunt that went with it, and the hidden word *fuck*. *Buick* odd-rhymes with *fuck,* which together say *ick* and *uck*. She was my friend, and she also appears in the dream "robin's egg" as the bearer of a toy egg.

I recovered a surprising and embarrassing memory around the time of these dreams. During recess, when the classroom was empty, I went to the blackboard, picked up a piece of chalk and wrote the word 'FUCK' in large trembly capital letters. Just as I was finishing up the κ, my teacher walked in. I was her favorite pupil, and I was polite, graceful, exact and talented. She said, *you* of all people. That was all she said. I was stunned too, and blushed deeply. Then I forgot I had done it.

As I mused over the dreams, the connection between the firetruck riddle and my writing 'FUCK' on the blackboard suddenly blared at me. I was solving the riddle by writing it out in chalk.

Much later, I understood that recalling the blackboard and the teacher—my sixth-grade teacher—told me how old I was when the events occurred.

It seems natural that I would commit this strange, lonely act soon after the firetruck/fuck phone call.

There were other dreams that bore a resemblance to the figure of the firetruck.

One was "sugar": the old red truck with the words 'SUGAR TRANS____ATION COMPANY' across the side. Just now, writing this, I see that the missing letters are an expression of the letters that fell out of 'FIRETRUCK' to make the word 'FUCK.'

In another, a small red convertible looking like a red patent-leather shoe is displayed on a gleaming white tile floor in the middle of a large showroom in midtown New York. The car is made of glossy red cardboard. I have to drive up the West Side Highway or the 'East Side Highway,' and I'm asking how to get there.

This wrong name for the East River Drive brought to mind a beautifully illustrated old storybook my mother read to us, called *East of the Sun and West of the Moon*. Rereading the story, I found that when the daughter tells her mother the secret of her love life, the mother betrays her.

I also noticed the red car on the white tiles—vividly, red on white.

Both the red Buick and the red-patent-leather-shoe car are 'convertible.' Something changes into something else: something is what it is and also something else: the way of the dream thoughts.

I longed to tell my mother what had happened. I dared. One evening after supper, I went to her room—which I rarely entered. Lying down on the bed, I began to sob, refusing to speak until she promised not to tell my father what I was about to say. Even now, I don't know which of the boys I named, or what I said they did. I don't know what I would have been able to say. We did not have a practiced way of talking to each other. I believe my mother never spoke to me alone.

She broke her promise, and on another evening soon after called me to the living room to speak with my father. The room was painted rich red, his whim (he also liked red shirts). He made a round circle with the thumb and forefinger of one hand, and a pointer with the fore-finger of the other hand, and pushed the pointer in and out of the circle, saying, did he get hard and then did he get soft? I bolted from the room crying and nothing was ever said again.

My father wrote a letter—saying what, I don't know. My father, a radical Quaker activist, spent his life writing letters. Some way, I learned or understood that he had written a letter to the fathers of those boys. Or maybe to all the fathers in the houses all around.

My mother also took me to a gynecologist—hers, I think. He put my feet up in icy stirrups—I remember his startling red face—and after probing me slightly, told her that my hymen could have broken from riding a bicycle or climbing trees. Both my constant occupations. I was still a girl, barely twelve.

◆

I never contemplated telling anyone else what had happened to me, even for a moment. Therefore perhaps the burying of the memories—too painful to sustain.

When I remembered again during the analysis, I knew that I had known. I find this of interest. When I remembered again, I remembered not only the event but also knowing about the event. And I also remembered the time that came when I no longer knew about the event.

I grew up without knowing why I was suffering.

Even many years later, when I was no longer young and had gone into analysis because of the cut attacks, I barely even hinted to my closest friend the reason for it.

I felt ashamed of the fantasies and also of the events as they at last began to unfold in my mind.

I lived always with the most exquisite sense of shame.

My analyst said I was 'ashamed to be alive.'

ROBIN'S EGG & PALE BLUE SHELL & V

"robin's egg": My friend Robin 'shamed' me by letting me know that she knew, i.e., everyone knew, that I had had sex. She didn't know that I had or if I had—and I didn't either. The egg—the pale blue shell of the robin's egg—represents the fantasy of the baby in my body and refers to the linked memory of finding a broken robin's egg with a dead baby chick inside.

Reading my notes, I came across the forgotten dream "pale blue sheets," dated only a day or two before "robin's egg"—a surprise foreshadowing.

"cord": I was troubled by this dream of tripping on the cord of a clothes iron, turning it over and over in my mind: I'm skipping, I trip on the cord, and the iron falls to the floor.

Going back to my notes, I discovered another dream featuring clothes irons: in it, two men are chasing me with hot irons among giant boulders.

I often found myself writing the letter V, and strings of words spelled with V, and then stumbled on the image of the V-mark burned into my pale blue shirt with the iron. Of course the V was also a triangle.

We lived a purposefully frugal life and had few new things. I keenly regretted burning the shirt with the iron.

I didn't understand that I may have burned it for some deeper reason.

The dream thoughts are full of runelike markings—an ancient language. But also a new, personal language: each person has one.

Here and there are glimmerings of something like the Jungian archetypes, or Joseph Campbell's thousand faces.

My pale blue shirt was a birthday gift from the other girl who was a player in the game. This may have been—I think it was—the shirt I pulled off during the game, which would mean that it took place sometime between my birthday on April 3 and the day I embraced the cat, which I knew was April 16. It was a pale blue sleeveless nylon top—these shirts were called 'shells.'

I've said that I forgot these events for many years. When I remembered them again, I also recalled the remembered date.

Discovering the connection between the pale blue shell of the robin's egg and the name of the shirt was a kind of eureka. It made me understand why the image of the eggshell and the color pale blue had been so riveting.

Among my mementos from childhood I found a poster I had made—with crayons on oaktag—in second grade: a mother robin and her chicks, and a row of ovals showing the progressive development of the fetus inside the egg.

The robin project and the name of my friend converged to create the dream "robin's egg."

When I dizzily imagined that I could be pregnant, I pictured a tiny coiled creature growing inside me. In this memory, I'm sitting alone with my diaries at my desk in the room I shared with two of my sisters. The room and the desk were painted dull pink. The coiled creature in my mind was also pink.

In the poster, the mother robin has a worm in her beak.

I learned, reading my notes, that my analyst had told me early on, in the first year, that I was suffering from a simulated pregnancy. I wrote this down and promptly forgot it. He told me again about three years later—again I heard him and forgot it.

The next time, I found the courage to ask how he had concluded that: he said that the physical symptoms that had troubled me over the years—amenorrhea, constipation, bloating, bulimic vomiting—all suggested pregnancy.

I had not yet assimilated the flashes of insight that came from the dreams or understood what they were saying to me.

Dozens of times I said to my doctor: And the cut attacks? What did we say they meant?

<br>

SPOON RINGS, JADE PLANT

My silver spoon ring has my grandmother's name inscribed on the inside. She told me once that her aunt Marion had been very lovely and sought after but had turned down her suitors and become a lonely old lady. This was a special message from my grandmother to me, because she had seen me turn mine away and then cry over them.

I didn't think the spoon rings were as beautiful as the spoons themselves, and would have preferred to be given the spoon.

The word *haft* emerged in the poem, which I don't think I knew was the handle of an axe, not a spoon.

My grandmother had beautiful silver hair in her old age: all pure silver.

In the next frame of the same dream, my mother gives me a jade plant as a wedding gift. The plant falls to the floor, and snaps at the base of the stalk.

My mother's gift to me, jade, being a jade.

## JADE RINGS, SNAKES, SNAKEPLANTS, GREEN SNAKES

A few days after the dream "spoons," I dreamed I was wearing jade rings on my toes—one or more on each toe, in many shades of green jade. I was in a book-lined room with a blond wood floor. Right away, I remembered another dream, set in the same room. In it, I was at a cocktail party, and a snakeplant was growing straight up from my skull.

Jade toe rings—a sequel to the jade plant.

Jadedness was heavy—the clunk of the rings on the floor. My sense of myself as a ruined person.

The plant falls and breaks.

There were many snakeplants in our house, those hardy thickets of dark green spears each lined with a single yellow stripe. I must have experienced myself as giving birth to snakes through my mind, and therefore the snakeplant is growing from my head.

For the first time in my life—dreaming these dreams, cultivating these thoughts—I found my own mind, my own self, interesting. If my mind can create such intricate and beautiful thoughts, I said to myself, I might be worth saving. I noticed that the dreaming mind was poetic, or moved like a poem, through suggestion and disguise.

The snakeplants brought back the terrifying childhood dream called "snakes"(1).

We lived in a great old farmhouse, with several fireplaces, and when we moved in as small children it had not been repaired or painted in many years—maybe as long as a century. The wallpaper in our upstairs bathroom was so ancient and so browned that its rose pattern was barely visible: brown on brown. As I gazed in the mirror at myself, brown snakes came crawling from the wall. They were wormlike, immense—and I ran naked across the lawn with them flying behind me.

Later, I had many dreams of snakes—relentless, I thought. In another not told in the poems, a gift box arrives full of clean straw, and reaching in, I pull out a handful of wriggling green snakes.

I recall a line from Frost's "Mowing"—'pale orchises, and scared a bright green snake'—a poem about sound and silence and creative work. This snake was not one of mine.

And yet, the next to last line of the poem, 'The fact is the sweetest dream that labor knows,' does have something to do with my dreamwork, working on my dreams to find the fact. Or, that is, both to trace their intriguing beauty and to find the fact.

There were clues I didn't see: in "green snake," the snake is pregnant. On my notebook page, I drew the picture of the boa constrictor that had swallowed the elephant. I reread *The Little Prince,* searching for understanding.

We sometimes found a small green snake coiled in the garden or on the lawn, and swimming in the pond, the boys held up long black snakes in the air like trophies, yelling *copperhead!*

One of those boys was the cat's younger brother, who tortured me in the basement, rubbing his snakepenis against my naked back.

Just now, writing, I notice—for the first time, after all these years—that "snakes"(1) expresses my wish to have escaped from him. Out of the basement and across the lawn—despite my nakedness. In the dream I'm running the other way, from my house to theirs, which may suggest some confusion about desire.

And what of the odd components of the word *cocktail:* a *cock* and a *tail.*

CATS & CATWALK

I've called the cat by this name because of the dream "cats" and the dream "catwalk."

Our families had many cats. They were always kittening, and sometimes there were dozens of kittens. The cats and kittens slept in the sunshine on window and doorsills and slouched across the lawns from house to house. As we children did, running in and out and upstairs and down.

As for the three cats drinking from the dish of milk, we were three sisters of almost the same age for three years before our younger sister was born, and I believe we were much in need of milk.

♠

My mother told me, when I was an older girl, still in my teens, that she had envied her brother, and envied his penis, and wanted to be a man. She thought of herself as a man without a penis. And eventually, when most of us were grown up, she left and fell in love with a woman, a relationship that lasted the rest of her life.

So I thought of her at once when the falling window sash lopped off the tail of the cat as it stepped through the window, getting away. A manx cat, I thought, and later the word *manxman* popped into the poem.

I just now learned, looking up the word, that *Manx* means an inhabitant of the Isle of Man. I had thought it was some variant of *manqué,* meaning missing something or not having what one wanted to have. This is a curious coincidence.

And isn't it odd, too, that the island is named Man.

There are many coincidences in dream thinking. They seem both random and mysteriously purposeful.

The figure—of a cat with no tail—bears an eerie relation to the lopped squirrel's tail. The snapped spoons, the snapped stalk of the jade plant. The snakes and lost penises.

And even maybe to my severance from the joys of a lived erotic life.

"catwalk" was not the only dream in which I observed walks and stairs reaching around a room, high up near the ceiling: stairs going a little way up and then a little way down. One set ran around the inside of a cathedral, near where the wall of the nave meets the slope of the high ceiling.$^{\Psi}$ Another ran around the inside of a red Renaissance courtyard. I saw the word *cat* in *cathedral*.

Years passed before I remembered that in the playroom of the cat's house there were ladders hanging horizontally on the walls, close to the ceiling. So this was the catwalk: we were up there in the ladders, having our tryst.

--------

$^{\Psi}$ I notice now that the interior of the cathedral in this dream resembles that of Saint Sabina at the Aventine, in Rome; read further for the riff *Sabino, Sabon, Sabine*.

One afternoon at the New York Public Library, I looked up the date April 16, 1966, and found that it was a Saturday. After long thought, I knew that a group of Quaker friends had come to stay that weekend. In the evening, after dinner, as I sat at the long dining table suffering my soul crisis, they were singing hymns and hearty rounds by a blazing fire. I especially remember *hallelujah—sing it over!*

Quakers often called each other 'folks.' Hello, folks, they would say.

So these were the folks in "catwalk," laughing and clapping.

PINK, PINK & WHITE
WATERMELON, HILLS
PINK PISTACHIOS

Although the fruit is pink-skinned with pure pink flesh and perfectly round, in the dream it is called a 'watermelon.'

Free-associating from the word, I remembered the fair at Strawberry Hill, where I was photographed eating a slice of watermelon.

The picture appeared on the front page of the local newspaper, a little blond girl eating watermelon.

Pure pink flesh—the pulp of a piece of fruit is called 'flesh,' and the name of the book that I was trying hard to remember had something to do with flesh: *fanny.*

At the same fair in an earlier year, my father knowingly or unknowingly bought me a used paperback of the porno masterpiece *Fanny Hill*.

I was an avid, precocious reader. Standing at the secondhand bookrack and opening the book at random, I must have been drawn in by the richly readable narrative. The word *hill* in both the book and the place where the fair was held is one of those startling dream-thought coincidences.

I was wearing a pink and white cotton shirt the day I was photographed eating watermelon, another coincidence.

The Tom in "pink pistachios" was the younger brother of some girls I knew. Manly and dark-haired, he resembled my father at that age.

The bush is leafless, bare except for the pistachio nuts, which are pale pink and as big as plums.

*Piss-tashio. Pee* and *mustachio*. My father's mustache and beard, pee, the scent of liquor and pipe tobacco.

After the evening I was called down to the red living room, I wasn't able to look at my father. I never climbed on his lap anymore.

In slang, nuts are testicles, this doesn't need to be said.

A tom is also the male cat: tomcat.

The black teddy with its red-pink flowers was a gift from one of my sisters.

I had wandered alone through the orchards in deep winter, where a red and pink sunset streaked the ice-heavy snow.

I'm half-naked on the ice, exposed—in the presence of—nuts, male erotic life. It seems simple. I'm cold and exposed and full of longing.

I had chosen the book from the bookrack in a sunny field; I had eaten the watermelon on a hill under some trees.

The yearly fair, which had always been held in a field, had been relocated to a wooded hill.

Therefore, the fair where my father bought me the copy of *Fanny Hill* had been held at least a year before the photo of me eating watermelon.

One evening in my New York apartment, I rummaged up the newspaper from a box of childhood papers. The date on the front page was 1964. I was ten that spring, which must mean I took the book off the bookrack the spring I turned nine.

Not long after—a year or maybe two—I came across a crumbling copy in a used bookstore and bought it nervously. Same red ribbon on gold. Reading alone at home, I had the sensation that *I* was *she*, Fanny; I was living *her* life; I remembered *her* seduction and betrayal as though it were my own. I knew the rooms, having assembled them long before in my mind—as we do when we read. The combination of arousal and anguish was so intense that I stopped partway through and set the book aside.

When Francesca turned up in "watermelon," I suddenly knew why I had always been so impressed by her punishment: an eternal embrace is something like my own psyche-damaging experience of lasting arousal both inside me and all around me.

BLACK, BLACK & WHITE
RAZOR SLASHINGS
CUT FINGER
WAR

"black chairs": my first thought was the lobby of the United Nations building with its huge glossy black and white checkerboard tiles—where I was working when I dreamed the dream.

Soon came the memory of the black and white check dress. I have always known that I was six when I cut myself. In a photograph taken that year I'm wearing the dress and we are all, my sisters and cousins, smiling sweetly for our grandfather's camera.

I had no articulated intention to harm myself, but I have reviewed the moment countless times and I believe the act was deliberate. I put my finger in the juncture of the metal pole of the swingset and the metal poles sustaining the glider swing, and let the swing go. Even saying so now, as I write, I crumple up, clenching myself.

♣

Waking from the dream, I felt as I had felt as a small girl, alone with my self-destructive act, uncomprehending.

I had never forgotten it, rubbing the scar like an amulet whenever I was in distress. The revelation comes in the line 'now someone laughs now all the others laugh.'

I told no one that I had done it to myself. I'm not sure I knew. I don't recall any expression of sympathy, which I deeply believe was what I wanted when I cut my hand.

In the kitchen, with my elbow propped on the big oak table and my gauze-wrapped hand in the air, I watched as my sisters carried on with their drawing and coloring.

The gauze bandage echoes the white lace dress—and of course implies that there was blood.

"black chairs" also illuminates the subway fantasy: my hand falling off and rolling away.

"black slip" = black *lace* slip. The word *décolletage*, a low-cut neckline, comes from the French *décolleter*, which means 'cut out the neck of,' as for a dress, and also 'cut someone's neck.'[Ψ] Here, I'm the wrongdoer, having stolen the slip, and I'm sentenced to a razor death.

In another dream not told in the poems, I'm walking on a path over a great lawn with many paths fanning out through it. Then I see a lovely young blond woman lying flat on her back on the grass beside the path. She turns her head to the side, and as she does, I see that her throat is slit and that blood is pouring out of it. She's slim, and she wears a tight, stylish black dress and a pair of black slip-ons.

When I wrote down the dream, I called the dress a 'sheath.'

How strange that a sheath is a dress but also the holder for a knife or a sword.

And a vagina, I had forgotten this.

"war" reminds me that the razor-slashing dreams are all about love—erotic love and self-love. I thought and thought about the L-shaped room, the L high above the river, before it came to me: L is love.

Isn't that the subject of all the dreams? Or of life: love, the life subject.

---

[Ψ] Also related to *décollation* and its English cognate *decollation* = decapitation.

The razors were anguishing, senseless. How could god, the gods, creators of life and dreams, inflict them on me in my sleep?

Lean, tan, blond: who was she slashing?

Any blond woman is me.

In "shiny foil," my molester—as I call him in the dream—is sentenced to be executed with a razor, but by the time I understand that his molesting is a form of love, it is too late to save him.

Just now, as I write, it occurs to me that *foil* also has another meaning, a literary one: isn't the molester a 'foil' for my own spurning of love and longing for love? A thing that contrasts with and enhances the qualities of the other.

And another: a 'foil' is a sword that doesn't cut: almost a story *en abîme* in a story about love.

Here again, *foil*: they were 'foils' for each other, the two brothers. I mingled them together, remembering. They harmed me; they hurt my life; they did me irreparable harm.

And yet, there was something *shiny* about me and the cat, as he bent his head and looked in my eyes—out there on the driveway.

I think the cat loved me, I said to my analyst.

Here I was, surprisingly, calling it love.

I was worried that he would be punished.
This came to me suddenly.

The cat shouldn't have touched me, I said.
No, he said.
It dawned on me that I had never named the cat's brother or the friend, the evening I told my mother. This confused me, I felt almost dizzy, trying to understand.

But *they* were the brutal ones. *They* were the ones who should have been punished.
Why didn't I?
Maybe I couldn't bear the thought.

Anyway, I never meant to tell.
Except my mother, I wanted to tell my mother.
No one but her was meant to know.

So who did I name? The cat—the three boys?
I had tagged along, down the hill and into the woods.

I don't know what I told her. What could I have said? I said almost nothing. I sobbed, sobbed. I said a few words.
So what could she have said to him—my father.

*Foiled,* my love was *foiled.*

I met, during my travels, a strikingly beautiful Swiss woman, slim, majestic, with big dark eyes and straight black hair—a Cleopatra. She was so lovely, so self-possessed that her anguish seemed mysterious and improbable. We talked for a while about ourselves, and found similarities. We were grief-stricken. Something had gone wrong when we were young, something sexual and invasive.

We had both cut our own fingers: mine the right index, hers the left. But as she explained, since she was a lefty, it was the same finger. The one that points, the one that writes.

I cut mine *before* the events; I don't recall if she told me when she cut hers.

Somewhere I've seen the sculpture of a sphinx or a Sekhmet with protruding ribs.[Ψ]

I discovered after writing the poem that *patra* does have the same root as *patria:* so here was the homeland of our souls.

There is something about pain that ratchets up the nerves, that makes us skinless and vulnerable.

---

[Ψ] I searched for the source of this figure: it was not at the Met in New York, but I found it at the Louvre—several sphinxes, big and small, with lean ribbed flanks.

"letter," as I say in the poem, is not about a dream. It's about the letter my father wrote, telling our neighbors what their sons had done to me. I want to say again that he can't have known what they did to me.

I have tried endlessly to imagine what he could have said.

"letter" features black and white, with my usual associations to danger.

I'll remind you of the corny old joke with its many replies: What is black and white and red all over?

Here are the three that appear in the poem.

—A newspaper = news of my shame being spread.
—An embarrassed zebra = my embarrassment. Stripes = I committed a crime and am punished.
—A bleeding nun. I might have written *penguin*, which is nicer—but *nun* has more meaning in a matter that has to do with sex, especially since the word is a homonym for *none*.

I'm reading the poem as though it were a dream. But some poems seem to spring, like dreams, from the deepest part of the psyche.

The poem says there was no dream, but now I remember a dream that came a decade before the analysis:

I'm reading a newspaper that's spread open on the oak table. Meanwhile, my father is painting the table with a paint roller full of bright red paint: fire-engine red. First he paints the underside of the table, then the tabletop. When he reaches the newspaper, he rolls the red paint right over it.

The oak table was beside the kitchen fireplace.

My father had a secondhand stand-up Underwood.

The old manual typewriters featured typewriter ribbons with a black strip above and a red strip below. You pushed a tab on the keyboard to get the keys to strike red ink instead of black. But when writing in black ink, if you didn't hit the keys hard enough, some red 'bled' into the bottoms of the letters.

In an odd backward way, writing the poem about the letter produced wordplay that calls up a dream that elucidates the wordplay.

The letter was *my* punishment, spreading the news of my shame like red paint.

POKER

I had no memory of the strip poker game until I dreamed of the tall banners bearing faces from a deck of cards—carried aloft on a dusty path through some trees.

Right away, I saw the path crossing the lawn between our two houses. It passed under some trees, and brought me to the door of their playroom.

The face cards billowed on the banners.

*The* KING, I said to my analyst—. Nickname of the cat.

Returning from the bottom of my mind was the cat dealing out the royal cards in a far corner of the basement, with last rays of afternoon light passing through the small high windows.

So the JACK is his younger brother.

The QUEEN is me: *I* am the QUEEN.

And then I knew that the snake torture—JACK and the friend pushing me against the furnace and torturing me with their penises—had followed right after the game.

I was surprised to see 'picket sticks' emerge in the poem—not a usual term for poles carrying processional banners.

Just now I found a pun in *poker:* poke her.

And in *banner,* an odd association: marriage banns and banning. *Banned.* So I felt. A royal disaster.

A picket is a stick, *and* a protest.

"leopard": When the leopard girl flew through the woods in her red satin bodice and spotted cape, I was awed by her glorious stage-girl beauty and panache. She was red-haired, so she wasn't me. But there were the breasts, just like mine, and my envy of her bravery and joy.

She's another cat, isn't she—a wild cat.

Sex seemed scandalous, necessarily secretive. In "red satin," a sort of opium dream, there are two men, and I don't know which is mine. This dream is one of countless dreams in which I'm with more than one man. Often, there are two men. My relation to them is uncertain. Often, I love one, but kiss the other, and therefore lose the one I love.

My dream imagery is sometimes dull and colorless, and sometimes extraordinarily beautiful in an abstracted way. Both "leopard" and "red satin" were intense, powerfully colored—much like the colors of a poppy.

♥

I was mortified that the cat would learn what else had happened to me. If others knew, I was sure he did too. But what did they know? I didn't dare ask.

Almost a year after the events, and just after my first menstruation, I called the cat's house on the phone one night after supper, pulling the long red cord down the front hall. Deep winter; there was a fire in the kitchen fireplace; snow was falling. The path had been shoveled out; we stood on it, facing each other. I sobbed, and told him I was sorry for *telling.*

This was my most bitter feeling: I had spoiled everything by *telling.*

By *telling,* I had lost not only the cat but everyone and everything.

The cat, all the other boys, all the girls—. All my thoughtless freedom. Even my mother and father were lost to me in a world of clumsy uncomprehending.

I have never again felt such immense life-sorrow, childish, hapless and ravaged.

GLASS CASES

Glass cases and other see-through glass objects appeared in many dreams, or emerged as I free-associated from the dreams.

It slowly came to me that these were representations of the incubator in which I lived for the first few weeks of my life: one of a pair of twins,$^{\Psi}$ I was born in 1954, a month early, and too small. During that time, I had no

———
$^{\Psi}$ A sororal twin—another story all its own.

118

physical contact with my mother: she stood behind the glass partition as the nurse held me up for viewing.

In "three vases," the rose heads are inside the glass vases, 'drowning.'

The rose pattern on the wallpaper in the front hall, a faded three-rose pattern, yellow, pink and blue. Hair flowing underwater, little girls with flowing hair—my sisters and me.

The fur teacup evoked in "squirrel" is in a glass museum case.

In "quarrel" there are vicious rat squirrels in a glass cupboard[Ψ] baring their teeth.

"cactus" recalls the small square glass box in which the Winged Victory's hand and finger parts are exhibited.[Ψ]

"glass case" describes a pastry case holding plates of excrement instead of cakes.

A dream is a sort of vitrine: even if you have seen yourself in the dream, you can peer through the glass but not enter.

---

[Ψ] Sudden thought: 'cupboard' may be—must be—an elision or contraction of the 'cutting board' on which I cut off the squirrel's tail, as well as a reference to the fur teacup.

[Ψ] I recall the glass box as holding the found fingers in fragments beside the hand; it was fascinating to learn, as I recently did, that the hand has always been displayed with the thumb and ring finger attached.

There were many dreams of shit, and toilets, that I haven't told here.

I dreamed of three pieces of shit in an orange pail in the dirty bathroom of a dark garage. The shit, the lurid orange pail, the number three all troubled me.

I dreamed of three stockings floating in a toilet bowl.

I felt offended by the dreams—insulted. The dream "glass case" was the ultimate offense, balking my wish to live with dignity and grace.

Joseph Beuys popped into the poem: I had seen a sculpture in a German museum, one crinkled sausage in a dusty, freestanding glass exhibit case. If there was another object in the case, I can't recall it.

It crosses my mind that the name Beuys is a near homonym for *boys*. I don't know what to do with the thought: it seems too clever.

I believe that "fruit bowls" was trying to tell me that the excrement in the dreams was only a figure—a construct. Maybe it was showing me that all this can be considered with some delicacy. The pieces of excrement are wrapped like fruit and seem also to *be* the fruit, in yellow, red and blue. I'm curious about the meaning of the primary colors—but no, this approach is too abstract.

It strikes me as interesting that these are the primary

colors, since the act of defecating is such a basic and primal experience.

My analyst would have said that this was 'not an inter-pretation.' He meant that it was a rational extrapolation, or in other words that anyone—the dreamer or anyone else could draw the same conclusion after studying the dream.

A true dream interpretation was personal. The dreamer followed a stream of thoughts—free associations—that only she could know: an irrational, non-sequential string leading to the memories that contributed to the creation of the dream thoughts in the mind.

I argued back: sometimes rational thoughts are freely formed in the mind!

Writing here now, I recall that the dream "shoaling"— the swarm of tiny swimming babies wrapped in toilet paper—unfolded in the place in the lake where one of my earliest memories occurred. I was standing beside my mother on the pier while she chatted with one of her friends. Looking around into the water, I saw my tiny baby sister drifting downward, with large bubbles emerg-ing from her mouth.

I yanked on my mother's elbow, and she jumped in and saved her.

My baby sister was wearing a bright yellow bathing suit, forsythia-colored.

This reminds me to say that dreams can sometimes release their associations long after the fact.

Also to say that all the related events of a life seem to cluster around a traumatic thought in the making of the dreams.

"shoaling" too is a toilet dream: the babies are wrapped in toilet paper, therefore they've been excreted.

About three and a half years into the treatment, I wrote in my notebook:

This week I've been reading Freud's *New Introductory Lectures,* and I see how incomprehensible they would be had I not had the experience of analysis. . . . For instance, the idea that a child imagines that babies are born from the rectum and sees the penis as a piece of shit *and* a baby. This is so peculiar and yet amazingly explicates my problem.


CAUSEWAY


I said to my analyst: Why am I struggling in the waves if the smooth water is so close by? I can *choose* rough or smooth: Why have I chosen rough?

He seemed disturbed: he did not believe that suffering was a matter of choice.

Reviewing my notes, I was astonished to find the young woman with her baby gesticulating to me from the deep water below. I had forgotten her; I had not even noticed the meaning-packed word *causeway:* find the *cause* and you will know your *way.*

## THREES

I don't know when I remembered the three boys. I know that I didn't associate the repeating threes with them, or if I did, I dismissed the thought.

It didn't occur to me until late in the analysis that the cat and his brother and the brother's friend were another triad.

The cat's family had six children, and we were also six. These were many threes.

My older sister and my twin and I were a triad. Three little girls, three roses, three vases, three tulips. If I imagined that the three boys really did have real sex with me, then my frightened tender mind might have imagined three fetuses.

Three fish. Three pieces of shit. Three pieces of fruit. Three smokestacks.

Three Chinese jars with keys in them.

There is no answer to the threes; the answer may be 'all of these.'

How could I have looked at the dream "mustang" and not thought of the threeness of the men? By then I was taking threeness for granted—or ignoring it. Instead I thought about the word *mustang*, the red and blue feathers, and the lock.

I heard the refrain *must hang must hang*, with its easy ambiguities.

Lock—cock. *Lock* rhymes with *cock*. A cock—a rooster—has red and blue feathers. The dream figures merge.

In the poem "three chinese jars" there are many keys—perhaps to this lock.

SNAKE VACUUM & MASTER BED & END

My New York apartment, on the ground floor, was at the end of a long narrow hall that was always dirty.

In "snake vacuum," the thick black snake snakes around my body, cleaning me with its tongue. The snake is hideous, and filthy. But it's not cleaning me, it's invading me with ugly eroticism—the penis made into an ugly, hateful and invasive tool.

Some dreams were so awful that I could not work on them in an interpretive way: instead of following my thoughts, I was overwhelmed by panic and revulsion. I suppose this *was* the free association.

Curiously, the healing symbol of Asclepius, the snake wrapped around a staff, is like this awful snake wrapping around my leg in a dirty hallway.

At the time I dreamed "master bed," I was so frightened by my dreams that I was afraid to sleep.

The master bed was my parents', in the front bedroom. My father slept there alone after my mother left him.

As classic as this dream may seem, it was one of the most disturbing. How could my analyst—the only one in the world who knew of these dreams—care for me?

I was so alone: I had been alone for a long time. A word joke comes to me: *masturbate*. The reverse of *master bed,* where the man and wife sleep together.

The ugly spate of recent dreams seemed endless and bottomless (I notice I'm echoing my poem "end": *there is no end & no bottom to it*).

PENISES

I had another penis-in-my-pocket dream around the same time as "big empty bed." In it, my sweetheart's penis has been cut off, and nothing is left but a couple flaps of loose skin. Then I find his penis in my pocket.

Through my dream associations, I discovered another

fold to these dreams: *I* was the one missing the penis, *I* was the one longing for sexual love.

As we all do, said my analyst.

LIPS & TULIPS & SHEER

"lips" seems to belong with the penis dreams—it came at around the same time. All are about important things not being where they should be. My lips are on my chest, right on top of my heart: these are both *mouth* lips and *sex* lips—attached to the heart. So here is a way of saying something so simple that everyone knows: erotic love belongs to heart love. I don't want to be a moralist, but this was an essential truth for me: I stayed alone for so many years, longing to be loved, and longing to make love.

Once late in the analysis, I told my analyst that I didn't want to have erotic feelings anymore: what good were they, they only made me suffer, they got me nowhere.

He said people have no choice about this, they have longings that need to be fulfilled.

"tulips": There are three *cutout tulips,* a word puzzle. There are three, there are three of *two lips,* they are *cut,* they are *cut out.* They are *lips.* This was one of the early dreams that stayed with me, bothering me. There was my longing to speak—in other words, to write—there was my longing to love—in other words, to kiss. And there was my incomprehensible self-cutting, and being ostracized: *cut out*. The tulips are red: here is the blood.

It became clear after a while that life's essential activities are linked to desire, and when desire is *cut off,* all the rest is also painful and impossible.

The dream passage in "sheer," with its riff *see-through, she-through, sheer* and *shears,* was a later frame of the dream of the jade toe rings ("snakeplant"). There were no shears in the dream: the shears are my association to the words of the dream. There's a way that both cutting and seeing go 'through.'

CAVE, FIRE

"cave": Fire shooting from my hands. I had to pass through myself: into my own sex—strange as this must seem—to be born.

I feel sure that I inwardly rehearsed the passage through my womb of an imaginary baby.

In the dream language, O'Keeffe's flower-vaginas and sculptural red hills combine in my mind to create this forbidding cave: the sexual self as the place where we become what we are.

Fire harks back to 'firetruck' and 'FUCK.'

The dream told in "airplane" led to the memory of burning my diaries; after "suitcases" I remembered how many there were, two or three; their colors, pink and white; and their gold details. Two white and one pink, or two pink and one white.

Writing "suitcases," I used the words 'burning . . . goldhot on the stones.' I was speaking of the sun. When I came to the last word, 'burned,' I saw that the sun burning on the hillside alluded to—suggested—the burning of the diaries.[Ψ]

Later I remembered what the pages looked like, filled from top to bottom and side to side with my tiny messy young handwriting, and saw them singe and refuse to catch fire on that damp day.

I wrote down hundreds of dreams. Some I reread and the rereading brought back no visual memory. Others stayed fresh in my mind for years, bothering me. One of these was "escalator": over and over I reached the top and

---

[Ψ] Looking over these pages, I'm surprised to see that both "watermelon" and "suitcases" feature the colors pink and white *and* the word *hill*; therefore, the figure 'hill' must allude not only to Strawberry Hill and Fanny Hill, but also to the hill I walked down with the three boys.

stepped off into a gold world: gold carpets, gold drapes, gold display cases: nothing that was not gold.

Saturated, pervasive gold.

And one day I remembered the gold furnishings in the living room of the cat's house. A flat, low, gold-colored couch, a beige carpet, and nubby gold curtains. Sand-gold, muted.


I wrote in my diary about what happened there and then burned the diary. The notion of guilt—as in the *feeling* of having done wrong—peeks out from the word *giltgold*.[Ψ]

A new doubt enters my mind: why did I burn two or three diaries if the events occurred within a few weeks—maybe even two or three weeks?

I have no answer for this.

I burned them all, banishing the past.


It was many years before I began to keep diaries again. Often alone, traveling alone, I wrote in cafés and train stations to keep myself company, and to make a record of my life. I had the idea that what I didn't write down would be lost, so I wrote and wrote.


The letters on the sugar truck were also gold.

---

[Ψ] I now also notice the 'guilt' in *guillotine*.

A single frame.

Navy-blue button lying in the street—my street in my grown-up life in New York. It belonged to a suit my grandmother bought for me, a handsome navy-blue suit with white pinstripes, accompanied by a navy-blue nylon shirt.

The shirt brings the memory.

My twin and my grandmother were nearby that spring day at the beach, and even so, when the sailors wandered over to speak to me I felt stomach-wrenching fear. Fear itself can be frightening when its reasons are hidden.

The word *gold* emerged in the poem, describing the sunlight and my hair, and alluding again to the gold-colored furnishings—or simply resonating with the word *gulls*.

Suit, suitcase.

## OLIVIA, OLIVE-GREEN CULOTTE DRESS, CACTUS

Here I was shipboard, with a wet wind blowing and waves beginning to surge across the deck. Hugging myself and crying out to Olivia, who had just told me that I must throw my suitcase overboard.

I often dreamed of losing the contents of my wallet, or the cards in my wallet, or my handbag. More than once they were swept away on a wave—once I found them again, mired in sand.

I hoped that Olivia would understand that there was something special and different about me: my suitcase was all I had.

Suitcases, diaries.

Why did I have so little? Intense pain and shame separated me from others, and from ordinary life.

Not until I dreamed of the olive-green culotte dress did I see that *Olivia* too meant 'I will live.'

I've always found it odd that the word *remedy* means both 'compensation' and 'medicine.'

I longed to have back my burned diaries and read the story that I burned up. The story is my self, my land. So "olivia de havilland" is an emblem of the analysis.

The olive-green dress was a real dress; one of my first sewing projects, I made it on my mother's old Singer—a sleeveless shift with culottes instead of a skirt. By now I was beginning to see—allow myself to see—the connections I was making in the underworld of my mind.

"cactus" is another dream using the same color. A small cactus in a clay pot—unlike any cactus I have ever seen. I was in the Louvre a day or two before the dream, and so when I sketched the cactus, I thought at once of the Winged Victory. I had seen her before, but never the small glass box holding her right hand and the found bits of her fingers.

*Her* right hand too, I thought, rubbing my scar. The poem surprised me with its wingspreading end—a kind of triumph over anguish. Look what she's missing, and she lived!

♦

That same day, there were milling crowds in the museum. Right by the Winged Victory, a little girl tugged at me. Slight and shy, she might have been nine or ten. *Madame,* she said tearily, *je suis perdue.* Madame, I'm lost. I took her by the hand and led her along the marble corridor until we found her classmates.

It's easy to forget how complex and intense are the thoughts of children, and how everlasting. I mean that the thoughts last in the mind, enacting their meanings, even when they seem to be forgotten.

Most dreams are secretive; some are blatant. When I dreamed "cary grant," I was still baffled by my mother's role in my world. I didn't see the pun in the name until writing the poem: it emerged as I wrote it.

As an interpreter of dreams, I agree that my reading of the shower poles as word clues may be overdoing it. As a poet, I've followed a sound in my mind.

Now I see that I may have cut my finger to elicit my mother's care: therefore, she was in a sense a finger-cutter. I was surprised by the ruthlessness of the dream. I didn't understand it—could not follow these thoughts down a path to discovery. The memory is disguised as thumbs and toes—so that I would and would not notice the connection to my own cut finger.

The mind gives up its secrets fitfully.

"rock" was a turning point. It forced me to take note that in my inner mind, my inner life, I did not believe my mother wished me well.

She was blandly nonchalant in her indifference to my comfort.

I did not know how unloved I was or that being unloved lay behind my acts of self-destruction and my vulnerability to damaging desire.

"snow" says this: 'I'd rather be hurt than left in the cold,' suggesting that I would rather accept love that hurts than have none at all.

♠

I ran into an older poet, for many years a mentor to me, on the No. 6 train while my mother was dying. He said that mothers are monstrous figures in our lives, and then tiny shriveled old ladies dying in a bed. He used the word *closure:* 'dying brings closure.'

In "knife," the word has mutated into *disclosure* and *closing.*

BELL

A bell rang and a head was smashed.
*My* head, of course, I said to my analyst.

The association to Carlo Carrà came later: a pale white abstracted head turned to the side against a night sky:[Ψ] modeling my own painful shying from life, my painful sense of flinching and being harmed.

---

[Ψ] It was odd to discover that this painting is called *The Engineer's Mistress* (L'amante del ingegnere), also a good name for my dream machine, with its bell, pulley and hammer.

The dream reflects an idea that my dark and terrible thoughts have driven out the playful, lyrical and poetic thoughts.

I didn't yet understand the role of darkness in lyricism.

Trauma smashes the mind: it stops us from thinking, feeling and remembering.

## CORNER & OH HELL

There were sudden glimpses of possibility and beauty.

The purple-silver sky, the row of buildings as a fan—purple, silver and forest-green. Gleaming and exotic.

The lover says, I have bought us a house.

The fan opens and shuts, and he goes off to sleep on a slope.

Love—consumed romantic love—any love—was slippery, paradisal. I have felt this all my life: fulfillment is near. And then it slips down a slope and is gone.

"oh hell" represents countless dreams of abandonment: the texture and wallpaper of my dreaming mind. A lover turns his face away, or jumps on a train, or climbs a hill and disappears over the crest. Over and over, a declaration of love and a sudden departure.

I barely knew the boy named Rusty Sabon who turned up naked in my dream; he lived nearby and was older. He was not a redhead and I don't know why the name. His lithe, auburn-haired girlfriend had the nickname Tiger; her name and her hair may have contributed to the creation of this figure in my mind.

Shortly before the dream, I hiked up Sabino Canyon in Arizona, where I saw a pair of large, gorgeous red cardinals: they were bloodred—surreal in their blood resemblance. The purpose of the dream—dreams do seem to have purposes—was to show me the way to the word *rust* and to an unlikely memory: the first time I menstruated I was distressed by the color of my blood. Not red, as I thought it should be, but rust-colored.

So the name of the canyon, the name of the boy, the blood-colored cardinals, and a notion about my own blood rusting joined to create the figure of the dream.

I remembered that I had counted up the amount of time that had passed between the events and my first menses, and had determined, in some childish twist of the mind, that my blood was rusty because it had waited so long to leave my body. I was mixing up the natural filling of the uterine lining (in preparation for my first menstruation) with my imagined pregnancy.

During the year that preceded the dream, I had seen the great paintings of the rape of the Sabines—barebreasted girls in flowing robes ravished by warriors, thickets of spears, babies. The word *rape* was linked in my mind to the word *Sabine*—and in dream life it found the name Sabon.

"hanger": Slowly, I dug from my mind an essential related memory: in *Reader's Digest,* probably at Sunday school, I had read an article about rusty-hanger abortions.

As I remembered—which I tried not to do—I felt a deep frisson in my sex, strange and shocking— extraordinary. In my imagined body, the body where I lived my thoughts, I had spawned and then buried a fear.

I was pregnant, I would need an abortion. I would have to risk my life to be rid of the baby.

Why was my blood rusty? My rust-colored menstruation derived from the rust of the abortion.

♣

Did I know then, at almost thirteen, that this wasn't true? I didn't know if it was true or false nor did I know that I had thought it. And yet, I *distinctly* remember having *vaguely* thought it. I understood and also didn't understand that I could not have been pregnant because I had not begun to menstruate when that tangle of events occurred: my body wasn't ready for babies.

Here also was the desire to be cut and the fear of being cut.

The incinerator was a rusty barrel.

It came to me after writing "mustang" that the spin-off words *must hang* could be a curtal rhyme for *rusty hanger.*[Ψ]

STONE WELL & SOUTH & STONE + WELL

Another event occurred, apart from me but also intensely inside my own mind. Late one night, a boy named Alan Stonewell, who had recently mailed me a page-length incoherent love letter, stabbed a girl named Sarah. The stabbing took place in his house, and in his room. I had been in the house earlier that evening with some friends, and I knew that she could well have been me.

As I jumped off a rope swing, here was the other Sarah, lifting her peasant blouse and showing me the scar, which ran from one side of her belly to the other.

---

[Ψ] *Roe v. Wade* was decided six years later, in January 1973—a few months before I turned nineteen—altering the psychic landscape of sexual life and lifting away the fear of harm or death associated with unwanted pregnancy—and partly also the shame. This is the political story that affects the private one.

We barely knew each other; she was a little older; we went to different schools—but we were in the same crowd, same world.

Rope swing, suggesting also "ropeladder," with its weird and distorted birthing.

The "stone well" fantasy first appeared in my mind when I was about sixteen—I may have been younger. I didn't know it was a bad sign; I didn't talk to myself about it. I coped by using the well stone to round up and hide the razors, which was hard mental work.

The razor swarms turned up only when I was alone, lying in bed, wanting to sleep.

♥

A point came in the analysis in which I felt I could go no further. I knew everything there was to know, or so I thought: I had rooted out the causes. My psychosomatic illnesses had abated, I was writing poems, I lived more comfortably and slept better: I was taking more pleasure in life. And yet, in moments of distress, I could still see the blades starting to push against my edges.

A year or so after the treatment ended, I read through my dream descriptions and the pages of free associations—there are hundreds of pages.

Reading some notes to a dream, I noticed that at the time of their writing I had dropped out one word in the name of a road, leaving an underline where the word belonged. It was an important road in my life, near where I lived; I shouldn't have forgotten it: South Valley Road, and the missing word was *south*. As an experiment, I tried free-associating with *south* as a starting point. First came a string of words arising from *south:* south, southern, sudden, slattern, soul. . . . I remembered a party, a picnic; I saw myself walking down the road, as I had often done. I came to the house where the Stonewells lived—a sixties modern perched in the woods above the road.

In an instant, I saw that the words of my fantasy, *stone* and *well,* belonged to that name and place, and were related to the stabbing of the other Sarah.

The disappearance of a word or a name may be a pointer: near here lies the clue.

I don't remember feeling fear when I learned of the stabbing. I imagined the act and remembered the love letter, feeling a twinge in my stomach.

Was the fact that I had ignored his letter, never acknowledging it with a word or a look, the reason for the boy's rage? I had no interest in him. Did he take it out on the other Sarah? I had had these thoughts half-awarely, subliminally.

Stone and well. I had corralled the delusional swarming razors into the well with a large flat stone: the well stone. *Stone + well = stone well = Alan Stonewell*, the name of the boy who stabbed the other Sarah.

Well stone, stone well.

So the fantasy that had disturbed me for so long was a riddle: the objects—stone and well—the old stone well in our backyard—were the clue that led me to its origin: the stabbing.

In creating the fantasy, my mind had transformed the knife into razors as a disguise: much the way a dream works.

My mind had invented the fantasy so that I could enact the ritual of burying my fear, which was too painful to contemplate.

The fear that I should have felt was hidden from me for more than thirty years.

The fear of the abortion and the fear of the stabbing had combined in my mind to create the cut attacks. And my cutting my own finger joined in: finger, shaped like a tail, or a snake, or a snakeplant, or a penis—or a knife. I must have understood that the stabbing was sexual: it was about sexual desire mixed with anger and aggression.

My sense of relief was instant. Knowing the origin of the fantasy—understanding the riddle behind the thought—abolished its power. It was as though a layer of darkness were lifting from inside me and vanishing. Again I was amazed by the poetic powers of the mind—my mind.

After a trauma, the mind weaves a pattern around it, collecting events from any part of life—before, after—to create the mental puzzle that forms the obsessive fantasy, the phobic experience.

Have I put together the pieces of the puzzle?

♦

In the years following the end of my treatment, I saw both Robin and the cat. She looked me up one summer, having read my first book of poems. I looked him up, trembling, and saw him out west while on a reading tour. I asked them both about the letter my father wrote. Had they seen it: what did it say? The cat said there was no letter—he had never seen it or heard of it. Robin said she had seen the letter in her mother's hands.

I asked the cat if he was punished. He said no, his father had told him that sex was powerful, and that he must always 'take care of' those with whom he had it.

'Take care of,' an odd word choice. He did not say 'care for,' meaning love.

His words or his father's, I wonder.

If there was no letter, how did your father know? I said. Your parents came to see mine.

He said something else: I knew nothing. I said back: I knew nothing.

I had a doubt: he should have known; after all, he had been fifteen to my barely twelve. And yet, the confession was assuaging.

He said he had heard the other boys cutting up—about me. (There's that word again: *cutting*.) He had tried to silence them.

He also said this: You kept coming at me, you would not leave me alone. I succumbed to temptation.

Temptation? A skinny little twelve-year-old—I barely had breasts.

Your breasts, he said, were breathtaking.

♠

I was the more hurt. I whisper this now, as I write, hearing an echo in the odd turn of phrase: *the more* hurt.

*I did love you once.*
*Indeed, my lord, you made me believe so.*
*You should not have believed me . . . I loved you not.*
*I was* the more *deceived.*

How surprising are the associative powers of the mind.

*Go thy ways to a nunnery. Where's your father?*
*At home, my lord.*
*Let the doors be shut upon him, that he may play the*
*fool nowhere but in's own house. . . . If thou dost*
*marry, I'll give thee this plague for thy dowry: be thou*
*as chaste as ice, as pure as snow, thou shalt not escape*
*calumny.*

I felt a flood of affection and desire; I felt all that I had
felt for him as a young girl.

So complex, the desire, the implicit criticism. As for a
poker game, he had no memory of that.

# index

The index is imaginative, not exhaustive. Page numbers in bold indicate that the entry is the title of a poem.

black slip  **27,** 110

black snake(s)  climbs up my leg 32, on refrigerator 51, held
  up in air 102, around my body 124

blackboard  92–93

bled (ink)  115

bleeding  nun, red ink 25; nun 114

blond (hair)  41, 57, 86, 105, 110, 111; *as* yellow 6, 11; *as*
  whitegold 35, *as* gold 130

blood  *as* pink water, bloodwater on altar 7; *as* brightpink,
  prettypink blood on shirt, skirt, hat 9; *as* brightpink blood
  on dress 16; on pale blue sheets 24; *as* badblood thought, *as*
  deepred cloud 43; *as* cardinals, red as blood / monthblood,
  color of rust 68; rusting 69, 136–138; *as* bloodthought 70;
  of my eye, bloodletting 71; *as* bloodrazor swarmthought,
  redbloodcloud, bloodthought, bloodlife 72; *as* bloodred
  caveplace 73; from slit throat 110; tulips 127

blood on white clothes  shirt, skirt, hat 9; lace dress 16, 88,
  109; chiffon (dress) 62, 71; eyelet dress 71, 88; man's shirt
  87; *and see* red on white

bloodletting  71

bloodspot  on man's white shirt 87

bloodwater  7, 87

blue  (*as* skyblue) egg 13; pale blue sheets, sky 24; navy,
  navyblue button, suit, shirt, jeans / *as* blueclouds, highbluesky,
  highwhiteblue / fear, air, sky 35; pale blue shell, shirt 44; dishes,
  jewels 45; jars 50; *as* bluerose 52; fruit 53; (*as* nightblue) sky 61;
  birds, feathers, sky 66; (*as* pink & blue) me 69; lace cocktail
  dress 88; pale blue shell, sheets 96; shirt, top, shells 97; rose
  119, fruit 120; feathers 124; navy-blue button, suit, shirt 130

147

blushed, blushing   zebra 25, *as* embarrassed zebra 114;
  I blushed 92
boat    58; *and see* ship
boys    *see* three boys; as homonym for Beuys 120
breast(s)    *as* lips on my chest, over my breast 34; *as*
  fingerneckthighbreast 42; *as* leopard girl's redbreasts, my
  breasts, redbreasted, red satin breasts 47, 117; sheared off 55;
  my newborn 69; *as* barebreasted girls 137; I barely had 143
brown snakes   8, 101
brownpaper wall    8; *see* wallpaper
buick    *see* red buick
bully   61
burn, burns, burned, burning    diaries 10, *as* sins 12, 22, 80,
  88–90, 128–129, 131; incinerator 10, 12, 88–90; firetruck
  14; shirt with iron 44, 45, 97; joy 47
butterfly   34
button   *35,* 130
cactus   *60,* 81, 119, 132
Campbell, Joseph   97
cardinals   68, 136
cards   36, 115–116; *and see* poker
Carrà, Carlo   61, 134, *footnote on* 134
Cary Grant   *31,* 133
cats   *18,* 102–104
cat(s)   three cats, *as* manxman 18, *and as* manx cat, cat with
  no tail 103–104; *as* wildcat, catpal, wild catland, catpot
  18; catwalk 21, 102, 104–105; *as* sphinx, bigcat 46, 113; *as*
  leopard girl 47, 117, *and as* wild cat 117; *as* tomcat 106; *as*
  Tiger 136; *and see* kittensoft

cut   *by* razor, guillotine, scissor, knife, sword 42; by razors, knives, swords, scissors, pins, guillotine, egg slicer 78; desire to be cut, fear of being cut 138

cut, cutting   fingerneckthighbreast, lipofsex 42; (*and as* sheared) breasts, herself 55; skincut, lifecut, soulcut, her 72; sex, legs, hands, fingers 78 *and see* cut finger(s)

cut attacks   79, 95, 99, 141

cut finger(s)   *as* baby finger 7, 86–87; my finger 26, 60, 87, 108–109 (*and* Cleopatra's) 113, 133, 141; *as* thumbs & toes 31, 133; *as* fingerneckthighbreast 42

cut off, cutting off   squirrel's tail 17, 91, *footnote on* 119; penis 125; desire 127

cut out *as* ostracized   127

cut out for   parrot tulip job 54

cut out the neck of   110

cutouts *of* (paper) tulips   54, 126–127

cutter   who is the cutter, secret cutter 42; *as* finger-cutter 133

cutting   words 42, edge 78, comments 79, self-cutting 127

cutting board   16, 17, 82, 90, *footnote on* 119

cutting up   my life 70; about me 143

Cynthia, Cinny   12, 81, 90; *and see* mother

dad   20, *and see* father

darkhaired / dark-haired   *as* executioner's jetblack hair 27; sphinx / cleopatra 46; Tom *and* my father 106; Cleopatra's black hair 113

de Havilland   *see* Olivia de Havilland

death   *as* you killed me 5; *my* razor death 27, 110; sudden death *of* man on the ship / *as* executed 28, 111; fear of *footnote on* 138

*The Engineer's Mistress    footnote on* 134

escalator    *23,* 128–129

excrement (*or* shit)    on plates 30, 119; wrap up like fruit /
    wrapped like fruit 53, 120; in orange pail 120, 123; Freud 122

excreted    babies wrapped in toilet paper 122

eyelet    *71,* 88

fair    19, 105–107

*Fanny Hill,* fanny    19, 105–108, *footnote on* 128

*my* father    bought me *fanny hill* 19, 106–107; *as* dad 20, Tom
    resembled him 106; sent a letter 25, 95, 114–115, 142; rages
    79; *man* named Ray *footnote on* 91; room painted red, hands
    94; painting the table red 115; lost to me 118; slept alone in
    master bed 125; *as* parents 143

*his* father    142, *and as* parents 143

filthy    me, in the hallway of the dream 32, water on floor 38;
    snake 124

finger(s)    baby finger 7, 86–87; my thumb & first & middle
    26; like snakes, shaped like a snake 37, 141; my finger *and*
    thumb & ring *of* the Winged Victory 60, 119, *footnote on*
    119, 132; of my shame 62; clenching my 79; my father's
    thumb *and* forefinger(s) 94; mine *and* Cleopatra's 113; *and*
    *see* cut finger *and* thumbs & toes

finger-cutter    133

fire shooting from my hands    73, 127

fireplace(s)    101, *as* blazing fire 105, 115, 118

firetruck    14, 92–93, 127; *as* fire-engine red 115

fish, fishes    white 16, 56, 123; *as* starfish 62; *see* three fish

flame, flames, flaming    airplane 10, 89; yellow sparks 12,
    (*as* flame-red) tulips, lips, job 54

neck    snapped at the neck 11; *as* fingerneckthighbreast 42;
    low-cut neckline, cut out the neck of (a dress), cut someone's
    neck 110; *and see* throat

nevermarriage    11

newspaper    photo of me eating watermelon 19, 105–107; red
    shame of being read / news of my shame 25, 114, 115; father
    rolling red paint over 115

Nike    81; *see* Winged Victory

nun, nunnery    25, *as* homonym for 'none' 114, 'go thy ways to
    a nunnery' 144

nuts    20, 106–107

oak table    my elbow propped on 109, father painting red 115

oaktag    98

oh hell    *5*, 82, 135

O'Keeffe, Georgia, okeeffesque    73, 127

olive    I'll live I will live 59; *and see* Olivia 131

olivegreen / olive-green    culotte dress 59, 131; (*as* same color)
    cactus 132

Olivia de Havilland    *58, as* Havilland 81, 130–131

Ophelia, speaking to Hamlet    143–144

opium    48, 117

Oppenheim, Méret    *footnote on* 91

pain    *38,* 82

paint    red 94, 115; pink 98

pale blue    sheets, sky 24; shell, sheets, shirt 44, 96–97

pale blue sheets    *24,* 96

paper fan    49, *as* fan 135

patent-leather-shoe car    93–94

path    36, 110, 115–116, 118; *and see* lawn

red   buick, phone, redface 14; sugar truck 15; stripes on fish 16;
   (*as* redpink) flowers, (pink & red) sun 20; (*as* freshred) blood
   24; shame, ink, letters 25; *as* deepred cloud 43; *as* redbreasts,
   satin, (*as* redhaired, redbreasted) leaper 47; satin dress, lace,
   lap 48; markings *on* green snake 51; fruit 53; (*as* flame-red)
   tulips, lips, job 54; splat of birth, hand, starfish 62; (*as* red
   & blue) birds, (*as* red & blue, red blue) feathers 66; (*as* red as
   blood, redfeathered) cardinals 68; *as* redbloodcloud 72; (*as*
   mudred bloodred) caveplace 73; stripes on fish, on toilet seat
   88; buick, phone, cord 92, sugar truck, convertible, patent-
   leather-shoe, cardboard 93–94; patent-leather-shoe car, buick
   94; living room 94; Renaissance courtyard 104; living room
   106; (*as* red-pink) flowers, (red and pink) sunset 107; ribbon
   on *Fanny Hill* 107; newspaper, zebra, nun 114; paint, ink,
   shame 115; satin 117; (phone) cord 118; fruit 120; (*as* red and
   blue) feathers 124; tulips, blood 127; O'Keeffe's hills 127; not
   a redhead, (*as* bloodred, blood-colored) cardinals 136
red and blue   *as* freshred blood on pale blue sheets 24;
   mustang feathers 66, 124
red buick   *14,* 92, 94
red on white   stripes *on* fish 16, 88; stripes of blood on toilet
   seat 88; car on tile floor 93–94; *and see* blood on white
   clothes
red phone, redphone   14, 92, *as* long red cord 118
redpink / red-pink, red and pink   20, 107
red satin   *48,* 117
red satin   my dress 48, 117; on leopard girl's breasts 47, 117

up 44; is a ceiling 49; background like a nightblue 61; he's
  going to lock the 66; awe at the 86; head against night sky
  134; purple-silver 135
slash, slashed, slashing   his eye 27, her lean tan face / lean,
  tan, blond, who was she slashing 41, 111; I was slashed 70;
  slash scar 71; *as* razor-slashing dreams 110
sloughing   62
smashes, smashed, smasher   head 61, *and as* mind 134–135
smokestacks   12, 89–90, 123
snakes (1)   *8*, 80, 101, 102
snakes (2)   *37,* 82
snake(s), snaking   smacks of 6; swarming from roses /
  crawling from wall 8, 101; climbs up my leg, cleaning me 32,
  124–125; like fingers, rubbing me 37, 102; pregnant, green
  51, 101; Frost's 'bright green snake' 101; held in the air 102;
  and lost penises 104; finger shaped like a 141
snake torture   116
snake vacuum   *32,* 124–125
snakelike   83
snakepenis   102
snakeplant(s)   *6,* 81, 82, 100–101; 127; finger shaped like a
  141
snapped, snaps   spoons 11, 104; jade plant 99, 104
snow   *64,* 134
snow   *as* snowingwhite, snowslow, snowslurred, snowcold 64;
  rather be hurt 64, 134; ice-heavy 107; snow was falling 118;
  'as pure as snow' 144
south   *70,* 82, 140
spears   of snakeplant 100; of warriors 137

# acknowledgments

Deepest thanks to my analyst,
Nathan Kravis

and, as ever, to my editor,
Deborah Garrison

a note about the author

Sarah Arvio is the author of *Visits from the
Seventh* (2002) and *Sono* (2006). She has won a
number of awards and honors, including the Rome
Prize, and Guggenheim and Bogliasco fellowships.
For many years a translator for the United Nations
in New York and Switzerland, she has also taught
poetry at Princeton; she now lives in Maryland,
by the Chesapeake Bay.

## a note on the type

The text of this book was set in Sabon, a typeface
designed by Jan Tschichold (1902–1974), the
well-known German typographer. Based loosely
on the original designs by Claude Garamond
(c. 1480–1561), designed in 1966 in Frankfurt,
Sabon was named for the famous Lyons punch
cutter Jacques Sabon, who is thought to have
brought some of Garamond's matrices to
Frankfurt.

Composed by North Market Street Graphics,
Lancaster, Pennsylvania

Printed and bound by Thomson Shore,
Dexter, Michigan

Designed by Iris Weinstein